On the Fiscal Impacts of Immigration

European University Studies

Europäische Hochschulschriften
Publications Universitaires Européennes

Series V
Economics and Management

Reihe V Série V
Volks- und Betriebswirtschaft
Sciences économiques, gestion d'entreprise

Vol./Bd. 3109

PETER LANG
Frankfurt am Main · Berlin · Bern · Bruxelles · New York · Oxford · Wien

Karin Mayr

On the Fiscal Impacts of Immigration

PETER LANG
Europäischer Verlag der Wissenschaften

Bibliographic Information published by Die Deutsche Bibliothek
Die Deutsche Bibliothek lists this publication in the Deutsche Nationalbibliografie; detailed bibliographic data is available in the internet at <http://dnb.ddb.de>.

Dank für die finanzielle Unterstützung dieser Publikation gebührt folgenden Sponsoren:

Linzer Hochschulfonds

Integrationsbüro, Sozialabteilung,
Amt der oö. Landesregierung

Institut für Kunst und Volkskultur,
Landeskulturdirektion OÖ.

ISSN 0531-7339
ISBN 3-631-53340-3
US-ISBN 0-8204-7656-0

www.peterlang.de

Gewidmet
meinen Eltern
Johann und Christine Mayr

Dank an

Johann K. Brunner, Rudolf Winter-Ebmer und Reiner Buchegger für hilfreiche Kommentare und Unterstützung in Datenfragen, sowie Ben Lockwood - für seine Motivation und großartige Zusammenarbeit.

Linz, September 2004 K. Mayr

Contents

List of Tables

List of Figures

Chapter 1

Introduction

Immigration, and its political and economic effects, has been and is again currently among the prevalent and hotly discussed topics in Europe and the rest of the world. Receiver countries of large net immigration are often struggling in deciding upon which stance to take on the (potential) immigration they are facing, ranging from the degree of restriction they put on immigration (e.g. migration quota, selection criteria) to the degree to which they are promoting the integration of immigrants into society once they are allowed in, both economically (e.g. the degree to which they are entitled to receive social welfare benefits) as well as politically (e.g. the degree to which they are allowed to take part in political decision-making such as voting).

The importance of the subject of immigration into industrialized countries is mirrored in an extensive literature. Part of the economic migration research is dealing with the question of 'Is immigration - and how much of it and of which type - good or bad for the host country?'[1] This question to a large part

[1]More specifically, one might as well ask, 'Does immigration increase the national income of natives?' or: 'Are immigration benefits bigger than the costs?' In the words of Borjas (1995), it would be, 'Is the immigration surplus bigger than the fiscal burden imposed by immigrants on native

requires an analysis of the labour market performance of immigrants. Extensive research - theoretical as well as empirical - has been dealing with the question of 'What are the effects of immigration on native wages and employment?' However, apart from labour market costs (and benefits), there are also public finance costs and benefits, which determine the economic effects of immigration on the host country. Yet, in contrast to the labour market side, 'the economic literature has not devoted sufficient attention to the public finance implications of immigration for the host country'.[2] [3]

In the following, we deal with specific public finance effects of immigration in two parts, one empirical and one theoretical. Chapter 2 analyses the fiscal impact of immigrants in Austria within the method of generational accounting, which allows taking into account projected demographic scenarios for both natives and immigrants. Since the latter inherently have different lifetime patterns of residence and supposedly have different earnings and benefit recipiency patterns, they will generally make an important difference to public budgets. Chapter 3 uses a political economy model to determine the impact of immigrant voting on the outcome of a (direct) tax vote, and therefore the level of redistribution. Thus, both the actual participation of immigrants in fiscal redistribution in the host country as well as their possible political influence on the level of such redistribution are dealt with.

In the remainder of this introductory chapter, we will summarise on some empirical and theoretical papers dealing with the fiscal impact of immigration on the host country, as these are the lit-

taxpayers - and how can it be maximised?'

[2]Borjas (1999).

[3]Obviously, there are important links between the labour market performance and the welfare participation of immigrants; therefore, questions dealing with the skills and the assimilation of immigrants do not only have important labour market implications, but also possibly determine the welfare participation of immigrants.

erary contexts that the two main parts of this thesis belong to. Further, we will review some facts on immigration and the current state of social (economic) and political rights of immigrants in Western Europe. We will see that the granting of social and political rights to foreign citizens is among the most contentious issues in immigration and integration policies.

1.1 The fiscal impact of immigration on the host country: empirical evidence

The impacts that immigrants can have on host countries are various. As mentioned in Coppel, Dumont and Visco (2001, p.15), the precise size and nature of the economic effects of immigration will be different for different native individuals and will not only depend upon the relative skills of immigrants, but also their volume, different immigration waves, settlement patterns and other characteristics such as sex, age, country of origin and legal status. Furthermore, the effects are likely to vary with the time that immigrants spend in the host country.

While there is a common fear of adverse effects of immigration on the labour market[4], empirical evidence is ambiguous[5]. Similarly,

[4]According to a quantitative comparison of parliamentary debates in a few chosen European countries (Austria, France, Great Britain, Italy, Sweden, Netherlands) during 1996 and 1997 by Wodak (2000), labour market arguments are among the most common arguments used by parties which are against immigration ('Immigrants endanger the jobs of the native population or take jobs from them.') In fact, it was found that 'Austria is the country where employment policy and questions of work are most frequently explicitly linked to immigration.'

[5]Empirical studies for the US fail to find evidence for an increase in unemployment due to immigration (see for example Simon (1989), Borjas (1990 and 1993), Friedberg and Hunt (1995)). For Europe, some studies report small negative effects of immigration on unemployment, at least in the short

natives also sometimes fear adverse effects of immigration on public finances and the distribution of income.[6] The concern is whether immigration places an additional load on social welfare, education, health systems and the like, which is not compensated for by higher tax payments - that is, whether the net contribution of immigrants to the budget is positive or negative. Comprehensive surveys of the many studies estimating the fiscal impact of new immigrants on government spending and revenues are Rothman and Espenshade (1992), Vernez and McCarthy (1995, 1996) and MaCurdy et al. (1996)[7] Results generally suggest that in net present value terms, 'immigrants and their descendants tend to contribute more in terms of tax revenues than they absorb via higher government outlays, but the orders of magnitude are typically small'.[8]

It is important to note that any attempt to compute the net fiscal contribution of immigrants will depend, among others, on the methodology adopted, the public goods and services considered, the demographic unit of analysis (individuals or households), the inclusion or exclusion of immigrants' dependents and the time period concerned. Static studies of the (annual) fiscal impact of

run (see Winkelmann and Zimmermann (1993), Gross (1999)). Empirical studies on the wage effect of immigration generally find that immigration on average has small negative impacts on native wage levels (see for example Greenwood and McDowell (1986, p.1767), Friedberg and Hunt (1995, p.42)). Jaeger (1996) finds that immigration to the U.S. during the 1980s had a larger negative effect on the wages of the low-skilled and a positive impact on those of high-skilled native workers. A similar result was found for Germany during the 1980s by DeNew and Zimmermann (1994).

[6]Further arguments that were found to be featuring prominently in parliamentary debates on immigration are: 'Immigrants and asylum-seekers abuse the system. For example they live at the expense of the taxpayers.' and 'Asylum-seekers cost too much.' (Wodak (2000)) Also see Dustmann and Preston (2000) for the role of labour market and welfare concerns in determining attitudes towards immigration in Britain.

[7]See also the special chapter on immigration and social transfers in OECD (1997).

[8]Coppel, Dumont and Visco (2001, p.20).

immigrants have been criticised for suffering from the methodological problem that a single cross-section of data does not take into account the whole life-cycle of individuals. Children who are current net beneficiaries will become net contributors when they participate in the labour force, while current net contributing adults will retire and become net beneficiaries of the public sector. Furthermore, the long-run cost or benefit of immigrants will also depend on the choice of tax and debt policies, which can shift fiscal burdens between current and future natives and immigrants. In order to obtain a measure of the true fiscal incidence of immigrants, dynamic analyses are required, which take demographic and fiscal future developments into account. These also allow to calculate the effects of immigrants on the long-run economic sustainability of current fiscal policies.

The method most commonly used for evaluating long-term fiscal sustainability is that of generational accounting. It uses microeconomic data on fiscal payment streams of a given year (the so-called base year) to estimate the present value of future net tax payments by taking into account projections of demographic and fiscal developments. The method was designed in the 1990s by Auerbach, Gokhale and Kotlikoff (1991,1994)[9] as an alternative superior to annual budget accounting and was first applied to the US[10]. In the following, many countries have taken on the approach to evaluate the long-term stance of their fiscal policies.[11] In particular, the method provides a means to assess

---

[9]For further contributions see Buiter (1995), Fehr and Kotlikoff (1995), Ablett (1996b), Murphy and Beard (1996), Diamond (1996), Fisher and Kasa (1997), Raffelhüschen and Risa (1997), Cattoir and Docquier (2000), Mazzafero (2000), Borstinghaus and Hirte (2001).

[10]Auerbach, Gokhale and Kotlikoff (1991).

[11]See for Germany: Boll, Raffelhüschen, Walliser (1994), Gokhale, Raffelhüschen, Walliser (1995), Besendorfer, Borgmann, Raffelhüschen (1998), Japan: Takayama, Arita (1995), Takayama, Kitamura (1999), Sweden: Hagemann, John (1997), Denmark: Hougaard, Raffelhüschen (1997), Canada: Oreopoulos (1996), Australia: Ablett (1996a), Ablett (1997), Bateman, Ablett (2000), Ablett, Tseggai-Bocurezion (2000), New Zealand: Auer-

the long-term fiscal impact of immigrants. Immigrants can be expected to influence the host country's public finances in two ways. Firstly, they contribute to population size, thereby helping to bear the burden of public goods and pre-existing public debt.[12] Secondly, they pay taxes and receive benefits according to their socio-economic characteristics such as skill, age at arrival, fertility, mortality and emigration rates. The question generally is whether immigrants can reduce the burden on natives given by a certain amount of inter-temporal fiscal imbalance.[13] Studies that have used generational accounting to assess the fiscal impact of immigrants are Auerbach and Oreopoulos (1999) and Smith and Edmonston (1997) for the USA and Bonin, Raffelhüschen and Walliser (2000) for Germany. The former find a positive, albeit very small impact of immigrants on inter-temporal fiscal balance in the USA. Thus, the authors conclude that immigration should be viewed neither as a major source of the existing imbalance, nor as a potential solution to it. Smith and Edmonston (1997) distinguish between immigrants' fiscal impact on the federal level, which is positive, and the state and local level, which is negative. Bonin, Raffelhüschen and Walliser (2000) find that the overall fiscal contribution of immigrants is positive if they resemble current migrant residents in their economic characteristics. Immigration can thus decrease the fiscal burden on natives. However, even

bach (1997), Switzerland: Felder (1997), Brasil: Malvar, Kotlikoff (1997), France: Levy, Dore (1998), Bonnet (2002), Accardo (2002), Netherlands: ter Rele (1998), Belgium: Docquies, Liegeois, Stijns (1999), Stijns (2002), Mexico: Sarrapy, Caso (1999), South Africa: van Heerden, Schoeman (2000), UK: Cardarelli, Sefton, Kotlikoff (2000), Spain: Bonin, Gil, Patxot (2001), Abio (2003), Norway: Gjersem (2002), Finland: Vanne (2002), Hungary: Gal, Tarcali (2003). For overviews of generational accounting studies see Kotlikoff and Raffelhüschen (1999) and Raffelhüschen (1999a). Also the European Commission's (1999) composite of studies on European Union countries including Austria.

[12]Of course, they would also diminish any existing net wealth.

[13]The government is assumed to have to meet an inter-temporal budget constraint stating that over the long-run, public expenditure cannot exceed public revenue (For more on this see Chapter 3).

high immigrant inflows are found to only partially remove the intergenerational fiscal imbalance induced by aging in Germany. Our own generational accounting analysis of the contribution of immigrants to long-term public finances in Austria in Chapter 3 yields a result similar to those found in the studies above. The net contribution of immigrants is positive mainly due to their favourable age composition. The orders of the magnitude, however, are too small to significantly reduce inter-temporal fiscal imbalance.

1.2 The fiscal impact of immigration on the host country: theory

Theoretical papers on the fiscal[14] effect of immigration are usually concerned with the question of whether redistribution becomes more difficult due to negative fiscal externalities arising with labour mobility. While the general notion from trade theory is that migration serves to allocate the factor of labour where its productivity is highest and thus generates gains from trade for all parties involved (both the migrant and the native population)[15], several papers[16] have pointed out net costs of immigration for natives when immigrants participate in the welfare state.[17] The notion is that arising tax competition leads to a loss in tax revenues and thus impedes redistributive policies.[18] In this debate,

[14]We are looking at purely redistributive effects, i.e. abstracting from expenditure on public goods and public investment.

[15]According to traditional trade theory (Heckscher-Ohlin), free trade and free migration both lead to an efficient equalisation of factor prices.

[16]See Oates (1972) and, more recently, Wildasin (1994), Razin and Sadka (1995), Wellisch and Wildasin (1996).

[17]The income distribution frontier with free migration would lie below the no-migration frontier when mobile workers are net beneficiaries from redistributive policy and thus impose a fiscal burden on society.

[18]For a survey on papers dealing with factor mobility and redistribution see Cremer and Pestieau (2002).

however, the role of the political decision-making process in determining actual redistributive outcomes is not considered. In the following, we will review several of those papers that deal with the consequences of labour mobility for the welfare state in a political economy setting, some allowing for immigration to change the demography of a jurisdiction itself (most importantly, when immigrants are allowed to vote).

Several papers have studied the effect of immigration on the optimal level of redistribution, using different methodological frameworks. In a pressure group approach, where redistributive policy is determined via the maximisation of the weighted sum of utilities of different groups in the economy, Lejour and Verbon (1994) show that labour mobility does not necessarily have a downward effect on social insurance. Mazza and van Winden (1996) show that immigration can increase the transfers and income for workers if the number of immigrant workers rises. In a direct democracy framework with majority voting, Cremer and Pestieau (1998) determine the level of the payroll tax for a chosen type of social insurance within a setting of tax competition induced by labour mobility. In Razin and Sadka (1999a,b) or Casarico and Devillanova (2001), it is shown that immigrants can exert a positive fiscal externality on natives via the pension system.

Together with the redistributive effects of migration, papers also often deal with the question of how optimal migration policies are determined - that is, whether immigration is favoured by natives or not, the level of migration quota or possible skill or capital requirements that are to be put on immigrants. In an early model of regulation by Shugart et al. (1986), immigration restrictions are set by a regulator who considers conflicting pressures of producers and workers. As a result, immigration restrictions are tighter during recessions and looser during expansions. For papers using the pressure group approach see for example Amegashie (2002), where the number of immigrants allowed into a country is the outcome of a costly political lobbying process between a firm and a union, Epstein and Nitzan (2002), where, similarly, lobbying between two interest groups determines migration quota. Kemnitz (2002) uses a pressure group model to show that low skilled immigration can lead to higher unemployment benefits. Further, he finds that a positive number of immigrants is only allowed in if the political power of the high skilled is sufficiently high, and that the political influence of immigrants is minimised. Using a majority voting framework, Benhabib (1996) derives optimal capital and skill requirements on immigrants from their effects on the capital/labour ratio.[19] Also see Söllner (1999) and Grether et al. (2000) for an explanation of native attitudes towards immigration in the same vein. Similarly, in Flores (1997), whether or not a country admits further immigration depends on its factor ownership distributions, together with the generosity of its transfer programs. Papers that focus specifically on migration effects on redistribution within the pension system include Scholten and Thum (1996), who look at how immigration policy is determined by a native majority which takes into account immigrants' impact on a pay-as-you-go pension system with a fixed replacement ratio. Also see Haupt and Peters (1998), who consider both a fixed replacement ratio and a fixed contribution rate, and Razin and Sadka (1999b). Tamura (2003) determines majority voting outcomes on quantitative immigration policy when immigrants have both intra- and intergenerational redistributive effects. Similarly, Krieger (2003) determines voting outcomes when there are three heterogeneous voter groups (skilled and unskilled workers as well as pensioners), for different pension schemes.

Finally, a related line of the literature deals with the way that the effects of a participation of immigrants in the political process determine the preferences of natives on immigration and

[19] Typically, immigration changes relative factor prices in ways that benefit the relatively capital-rich and harm the relatively capital-poor, since immigrants are usually assumed to be capital-poor themselves.

on immigrant voting rights. When immigrants are allowed to vote over fiscal policy, natives must take into consideration how immigration affects the identity of the median voter over redistributive taxes and transfers. Razin et al. (1998) show that the participation of unskilled immigrants in majority voting on the level of income redistribution does not necessarily imply higher redistribution because of natives joining the anti-tax coalition.[20] In Cukierman et al. (1993), natives vote on immigration, taking into account that immigrants are attracted by both pecuniary opportunities as well as their influence on the outcome of a majoritarian political decision. As a result, the median voter may have an interest in delaying political rights for immigrants. Similarly to our own analysis in Chapter 2, Dolmas and Huffman (2003) provide a model in which equilibrium immigration and taxation policies are determined by majority voting. It is shown that, when immigrants are relatively poor (that is, they have no capital), a relatively poor native median voter prefers a low level of immigration, while a relatively rich native median voter prefers a high level of immigration. This is mainly due to immigrants' effect on factor prices. An enfranchisement of immigrants does not change a relatively poor native median voter's desired level of immigration. However, it decreases the level of immigration desired by a relatively rich native median voter, due to the higher taxes which result when immigrants are enfranchised.

In our model in Chapter 2, immigrants can be both unskilled (or, in terms of Dolmas and Huffman, relatively poor, and thus in favour of redistribution) or skilled (relatively rich). Natives' preferences on immigration depend on whether immigrants are allowed to vote or not. It is shown that an unskilled native median voter prefers a high level of immigration if immigrants are skilled. However, she would vote against immigration if immigrants are allowed to vote and the native unskilled majority is

[20]This result arises because, with endogenous education, unskilled immigration leads to more of the natives becoming skilled and, therefore, voting for lower taxes.

not strong enough.[21] A skilled native median voter is indifferent towards immigration but, for the same reason as before, will object immigrant voting if the native skilled majority is not strong enough. The issue of native preferences towards immigrant voting is interesting, since in most countries, while immigrants are granted social rights (such as the receipt of government transfer payments), they are granted voting rights only after a lengthy process of naturalisation. For more on this see Sections 1.3.2 and 1.3.3 in the remainder of this introduction.

1.3 Some facts on immigration

Migration has been of concern to countries all over the world at all points in time. In Western Europe more recently, post-war immigration, particularly that of migrant workers in the 1960s and 1970s, created large communities of long-settled foreign citizens. Furthermore, with the adoption of the Treaty of Rome (1957) by the European Community member states by 1 January 1993, European citizens became free to move, reside and work anywhere within the new common market. Fears of mass immigration from the former Soviet Union and Eastern Europe have been raised with the fall of the Iron Curtain in 1989 and the prospect of ten new member countries joining the European Union by 1 May 2004. Finally, the term 'fortress Europe' signals the perception of a threat from immigration from other continents such as Africa and Asia. The following review of the quantitative importance of and the main reasons for immigration largely draws on Coppel, Dumont and Visco (2001). The definition of immigrants used henceforth is the one of 'non-citizen legal residents' - along with the common definition used in most European countries of 'persons who move to a country and reside there for longer than a

[21] It is shown that, for heterogeneous skill compositions of natives, multiple voting equilibria on the tax rate can arise. In this case, immigrants' votes could change the equilibrium tax rate to the detriment of natives.

specified period that is often quite short, usually from three to six months'.[22]

A rough impression of the magnitude of immigrant stocks and flows world-wide is given by the fact that approximately 100 million people in the world live in a country other than their own.[23] In the OECD area (where data were available) alone, the stock of the foreign population rose by over 13 million between 1988 and 1998, to reach nearly 57 million persons, or 7 percent of the total population. In Europe, the proportion is relatively low at about 5 percent in 1998, compared with around 20 percent in Australia and Canada and nearly 10 percent in the United States.[24] Table 1 shows immigrants as a percentage of the population in selected OECD countries in 1981, 1991 and 1998. Within Europe, immigrant population percentages are found to be highest in Austria, Belgium, Luxembourg, Switzerland and West Germany with more than 8 percent in 1998.[25] [26]

While policies on immigration vary across countries and in general, two different schemes can be distinguished. In Australia, Canada, New Zealand and the U.S., 'permanent' resident or settlement systems are in place, which are typically based on specific selection criteria. In Europe, and also Japan and Korea, immigrants commonly enter through 'temporary' permit systems (even if they often remain in the host country indefinitely or for long periods of time). Different attitudes in immigration policies are also reflected in the application of citizenship acquisition poli-

[22]Layton-Henry (1990, p.5).

[23]Friedberg and Hunt (1995, p.25).

[24]Coppel, Dumont and Visco (2001, p.9).

[25]In interpreting migration data, one needs to be cautious and bear in mind the statistical caveats (see Coppel, Dumont and Visco (2001, p.6) for problems with definitions and comparability of migration statistics across countries).

[26]Also, one has to bear in mind that official data may underestimate the level of migration due to the movements of illegal or clandestine immigrants (see Coppel, Dumont and Visco (2001, p.10) for an estimation of illegal immigration to the U.S., Europe, Japan and Australia).

Table 1.1: Immigrants as a percentage of the population.

	1981	1991	1998
Australia	20.6	22.7	23.4
Austria	3.9	6.6	9.1
Belgium	9.0	9.2	8.7
Canada	16.1	15.6	17.4
Denmark	2.0	3.3	4.8
Finland	0.3	0.7	1.6
France	6.8	6.3	na
West Germany	7.5	8.2	8.9
Italy	0.6	1.5	2.1
Luxembourg	26.1	28.4	35.6
Netherlands	3.8	4.8	4.2
Norway	2.1	3.5	3.7
Spain	0.5	0.9	1.8
Sweden	5.0	5.7	5.6
Switzerland	14.3	17.1	19.0
United Kingdom	2.8	3.1	3.8
United States	6.2	7.9	9.8

Notes: 1. 1991 is 1990 for France, West Germany, Luxembourg and the U.S. 1981 is 1986 for Canada, 1982 for France, 1984 for the UK and 1980 for the U.S.
2. People are defined to be immigrants according to their nationality (European countries, Japan) or the fact that they are foreign-born (Australia, Canada, United States).
Sources: OECD (1994) and National Statistical Institutes (1998 data).

cies, which are either more liberal or protectionist. In the U.S. and Great Britain, the basic principle of jus soli is dominant, where persons are considered to be citizens if they are born in the national territory. It is also dominant in France, the Netherlands and Belgium either directly by acquisition of citizenship at majority (automatically or by option) for aliens born in the country, or under the form of 'double jus soli' where children born in the country, having one parent also born in the country, are citizens. In Germany, Switzerland and Sweden, for example, jus sanguinis is prevalent, and citizenship is reserved to those descended from earlier citizens. Here, the children of foreigners can only acquire citizenship by naturalisation, even if they were born in the country.[27]

In nearly all OECD countries the majority of new arrivals is due to family reunification, but the volume of asylum seekers has increased in many OECD countries over the past decade. The third main category of immigrants is those who come primarily to work. As to the skill characteristics of the foreign population, educational attainment levels of immigrants have been below those of natives in many OECD countries in the past, possibly also due to active immigration policies aiming at the attraction of low-skilled labour (see Table 1.2).

[27] De Rham in Layton-Henry (1990, p.172).

Table 1.2: Foreign and national adult populations classified by level of education in selected OECD countries[a].

	1995-98 average, percentages					
	Lower secondary		Upper secondary		Third level	
	Foreigners	Nationals	Foreigners	Nationals	Foreigners	Nationals
United States[b]	35.0	15.7	24.1	35.0	40.9	49.3
Germany	48.5	13.2	37.0	62.2	14.4	24.6
France	63.3	33.4	22.9	45.4	13.8	21.1
Italy	47.1	56.3	38.3	34.3	14.6	9.3
United Kingdom	65.1	43.9	14.7	32.5	20.2	23.7
Canada[c]	22.2	23.1	54.9	60.3	22.9	16.6
Sweden	30.8	20.4	41.5	50.3	27.7	29.3

[a] The educational attainment classification is defined as follows: lower secondary refers to pre-primary education or none, primary or lower secondary; upper secondary refers to upper secondary education or post-secondary non tertiary education; third level refers to tertiary education.
[b] Foreign-born and native populations aged 25 and over. Lower secondary refers to less than high school diploma, upper secondary refers to high school diploma, and third level refers to some college or more.
[c] Foreign-born and native populations aged 25 to 44. Lower secondary refers to below grade 9, upper secondary refers to grades 9 to 13, and third level refers to some post-secondary education plus university degrees.

Table taken from: Coppel et al. (2001), p.11.

1.3.1 The principal reasons for immigration

There are many and complex factors operating both in the host and the source countries that have an influence on the expected economic costs and benefits of immigrating. However, there is a common distinction between supply side factors ('push' factors) that affect the interest and willingness to emigrate and demand side factors ('pull' factors) that affect the demand for immigrants in the destination country.

On the demand side, there can be a specific need for certain types of workers in the host country, as mentioned in the previous section above. This was most notably the case between the mid 1950s and the early 1970s where widespread labour shortages led to the active promotion of immigration from migrant workers to Western Europe and Australia, for example. In recent years, host country labour demand has shifted towards skilled workers such as technicians and engineers due to prevailing labour shortages in the information, communication and technology industries in many industrialised countries.

Supply side-wise, relative expected incomes between host and source countries are generally thought to be an important factor influencing the incentive to migrate. Table 1.3 displays the proportion of average per capita income in the source countries (where the data were available) relative to the host country. Income discrepancies thus measured (that is, ignoring differences in income distribution within source and host countries) are quite pronounced. In nearly half of the listed OECD countries, the average annual per capita income in 1997 of the source countries is less than half the level of the host country, and the average for all the countries shown is close to two thirds. The income difference seems to be especially large for immigrants to the U.S. However, this calculation excludes primarily skilled temporary migrant workers, so-called 'non-immigrants'.

There are some qualifications to consider, however, when assuming a close correspondence between relative income discrepancies and actual migration movements. Firstly, the measure of relative incomes for a given year does only very incompletely represent expected lifetime costs and benefits of the migrant, which is considered by some researchers as the more relevant concept when assessing the incentive to migrate.[28] Secondly, actual immigration crucially depends on the immigration policy of the destination country ('demand factors'). Finally, non-economic factors are very important as well. Psychological stress associated with moving to another country, language and cultural differences and the (non-)existence of migrant networks in the host country all contribute to non-economic costs or benefits of migration that have been found likely to influence decisions about migration.

[28] Vishwanath (1991), Burda (1995).

Table 1.3: Per capita income in source relative to host countries in current PPP $, 1997[a].

Host country	Average number of immigrants (thousands)	Percent of total immigrants included in calculation	Weighted source country GDP per capita in 1997, PPP$	Ratio of source country GDP per capita to host country GDP per capita in 1997
Australia	87.4	66.6	12265	60.7
Belgium	51.2	74.1	17688	77.7
Canada	207.3	48.6	9900	44.0
Denmark	26.1	33.4	16679	70.4
Finland[b]	7.8	61.2	8744	43.4
France	77.5	55.3	6231	28.3
Germany	679.3	49.9	10016	47.1
Italy[c]	111.0	67.4	8279	40.8
Japan	243.9	67.3	10387	43.2
Netherlands	75.6	43.2	15497	73.4
Norway	18.0	61.7	17565	71.8
Sweden	33.6	32.6	17835	90.1
Switzerland	77.5	50.4	19262	76.3
United Kingdom[b]	219.8	89.4	14832	71.5
United States	773.8	77.8	6371	22.0

[a] Based on immigration flows between 1995-98. [b] Immigration data refer to average 1995-97. [c] Immigration data refer to 1998 only. Sources: OECD International Migration Database; World Bank Development Indicators, 1999. Table taken from: Coppel, Dumont and Visco (2001, p.13)

1.3.2 The social rights of immigrants

In Layton-Henry (1990, pp. 11), social rights are defined to 'include the right to a minimum standard of living and to share in economic welfare and social security benefits, general educational and health provision'. They are ranked second to last in a ranking of rights of foreigners by ease of access, only topped by political rights in the length of stay that is required in order to obtain them. While social rights are usually granted after a certain time after admission to the country, political rights are usually obtained only with naturalisation.

Comparative evidence on the legal entitlement and actual participation of non-citizens in host countries' welfare systems is hard to obtain and, according to Baldwin-Edwards (1997), it is 'perhaps one of the most complex yet under-researched areas of contemporary policy.' Social rights for foreign citizens in the European Union are often regulated in bilateral labour recruitment agreements which grant social security equality with nationals[29] or multilateral conventions governing migrants' social rights including the European Convention on Human Rights (ECHR) as the most significant one.[30] They differ according to the legal status and the nationality of the migrant. Thus, according to a survey on European Union countries in Baldwin-Edwards (1997), education and health services are most generally available, even to illegal immigrants. Unemployment benefits are generally available if the migrant satisfies the conditions of the scheme, while (means-tested) is rarely available and can threaten the residence status of the applicant, and public housing is sometimes available in principle, but hard to obtain in practice. Therefore, it is concluded that the best-protected migrants are Convention status refugees and those with permanent residence rights, so-called denizens, followed by workers and illegal immigrants who are the least protected.

[29]See Baldwin-Edwards (1991, p.195) for a detailed analysis.
[30]See Baldwin-Edwards (1997).

Social rights protection of non-EU immigrants therefore is far from unified across the EU and does not only vary greatly between countries, but also between legal statuses of the migrants and their different nationalities, even though 'suggestions of extending the EU co-ordinating rules on social security to third country nationals are now being made.'[31]

At the national level, 'the trend of governments has been to diminish the rights of (legal) migrants' as exemplified by the case of Austria, where in June 1996, all bilateral social security agreements with Yugoslavia, Tunisia and Turkey were cancelled on the ground that they were too expensive.[32] It seems to be true that 'in all European states there is some resentment that foreigners, and especially recent immigrants should benefit from the health and social security provision that the modern welfare state bestows on its citizens'.[33]

According to Freeman in Layton-Henry (1990), this implied 'membership scheme' of the welfare state that is reserved to citizens is justified on economic grounds. He argues that 'the international state system is marked by considerable economic inequalities, so that some states can afford much higher welfare benefits and socially determined living standards than the rest of the world. The very existence of such unequal benefits is a stimulus to migration, but unlimited migration would undermine the high level of these benefits. Therefore migration has to be controlled if these socially determined privileges are to be maintained. The principles of distributive justice need to be legitimised on a basis of solidarity that comes from common membership of a human community. The benefits of the welfare state are thus normally restricted to citizens, and non-citizens may be wholly or partially excluded'.[34] In other words, immigration control is seen

[31] Baldwin-Edwards (1997).
[32] Baldwin-Edwards (1997).
[33] Layton-Henry (1990, p.16).
[34] Layton-Henry (1990, p.12).

to be necessary for maintaining high living standards and social welfare benefits.

This corresponds to the finding in economic theory that labour mobility hinders redistributive policies: since individuals will, other things equal, have an incentive to locate in a jurisdiction with relatively wealthy residents where they can consume public benefits for relatively smaller tax payments, there will be a tendency towards a distortion in the allocation of resources in the form of inefficient migration into relatively wealthy communities.[35]

On the other hand, the taxation of foreigners might legitimise entitlement to welfare benefits, even if they lack membership in the form of citizenship. 'Those who contribute towards financing the welfare state should be entitled to its benefits. This would include foreign citizens who pay taxes and who therefore should be recognised as members of the welfare state'.[36]

Indeed, foreign (legal) residents are normally given the economic duties and rights of working and contributing to and (to varying degrees) receiving welfare benefits. However, they are generally excluded from political decision-making and therefore from decisions on how (much) taxes are to be paid and benefits are to be spent.[37]

1.3.3 The political rights of immigrants

Political rights are defined to be the 'rights to participate in the exercise of political power and the decision-making process, the most obvious means being by voting in local and national

[35] Oates (1972, p.83).

[36] Baldwin-Edwards (1997).

[37] Also compare Guiraudon (in: Joppke (1998, p.272)), stating that welfare benefits for foreigners in western Europe were secured early on while political rights remain contested.

elections, for local and regional councils and the national government'.[38] Full political rights are usually not immediately granted to immigrants. The common prerequisite for immigrants to take part in not only local and regional, but also national parliamentary elections is naturalisation.[39] There has been much debate on how appropriate this is, especially for long-settled, permanent residents of a foreign nationality who have become full members of their chosen country in every way except for the right to vote. They participate in the labour markets of the country, contribute to social security and receive benefits in turn, but as non-citizens they are not entitled to full political rights. For example, according to Layton-Henry (1990, p. 24), in Europe, the post-war migration of workers who have become permanent settlers without applying for citizenship has led to the presence of large numbers of residents who are excluded from political decision-making, making representative government no longer representative. A general trend in the post-war period is identified that gradually extends social, civil and also political rights to migrant workers and their dependants; as an example, the German laender of Schleswig-Holstein and Hamburg are mentioned, which have granted local voting rights to foreign residents. In the current European Union, five countries (Denmark, Finland, Ireland, Netherlands, and Sweden) out of all fifteen member states automatically deliver voting rights to non-EU immigrants, usually at the local level. However, none does so at the national level, where the level of redistribution is to a large part determined. In most cases, even local voting rights are a hotly debated issue, examples being Vienna, where the proposed introduction of voting rights after five years of continuous residency has been highly criticised by the conservatives and the Freedom Party, or the Belgian Senate, where the same proposal was rejected in March 2002.

[38] Layton-Henry (1990, p.11).
[39] See Layton-Henry (1990, pp.1).

What about EU-citizens? The Treaty on the EU states that every national of a member state is automatically citizen of the EU (art. 8). European citizenship provides, among others, the rights to move and reside freely within the EU and the right to vote and stand in local and European Parliamentary elections in the citizen's place of residence. (Exceptionally, a longer period of residency may be required if more than 20 per cent of the total population eligible to vote are non-nationals, as it is the case in Luxembourg.)[40]

However, whereas voting rights for the European Parliament are guaranteed (Council Directive 93/109), local voting rights are not uniformly regulated yet. Foreign citizens from the EU have local voting rights, for instance, in Denmark, Ireland, the Netherlands and Sweden. However, the European Court 'has the authority to rule an extension of the right to vote and stand for elective office in national elections if it can be demonstrated that lack of political rights is a barrier to movement'.[41] Political participation at the national level in a state of which the individual is not a national is 'intentionally excluded from the rights attaching to citizenship of the Union.'[42]

Immigrants, even if they are EU-citizens or long-settled migrant workers from the 1960s and 1970s, are therefore denied political rights to a large degree. Most importantly, they are not granted voting rights at the national level.[43]

---

[40] EUROPA (2003).

[41] Mazza and van Winden (1996), p.354.

[42] Guild in: Cesarani and Fulbrook (1996, p.37).

[43] At the same time, it has become harder for potential immigrants to be admitted. 'Since the end of the post-war European boom in 1973, labour recruitment has been severely controlled in all the advanced industrial countries of Western Europe, and in some cases it has been reversed. As labour recruitment has declined, there has been considerable increase in concern about the numbers of people seeking asylum in Western Europe, particularly from the Third World. This has resulted in the introduction of greater restrictions on the rights of people claiming the status of refugees. This is partly because some European governments claim that many asylum seek-

This fact seems to be rather puzzling and inconsistent, and yet it is true that 'even in those countries which have led the way in extending voting rights to foreign migrant workers, reformers have found a deep-seated resistance to the granting of national voting rights to foreign residents'.[44] What might be the reason for this finding? In Layton-Henry (1990, p.16), it is suggested that 'participating in parliamentary elections might be of great symbolic importance as a national political act that citizens are not prepared to allow easily for people unwilling to take the positive step of becoming a member of the national community through the process of naturalisation'.

However, even if foreign citizens are willing to change their nationality, it is not necessarily easy for them to do so. Naturalisation laws differ and can be more or less restrictive. According to Layton-Henry (1990, p.15), 'the willingness of West European democracies to grant citizenship to migrant workers varies considerably'. Naturalisation is relatively easy to obtain in Belgium, Denmark, France (especially for the second generation of foreign migrant workers), Ireland, the Netherlands and Norway.[45] Of those countries, Ireland, Denmark and the Netherlands have also extended local voting rights to foreign citizens. In Great Britain, the acquisition of citizenship was traditionally easy, but was made more difficult, and social rights were tied more closely to citizenship. Only Commonwealth citizens enjoy full political rights. Naturalisation is difficult and partly expensive to obtain

---

ers are not political refugees at all, but economic refugees - that is, they are really migrant workers unable to obtain entry and employment permits.' (Layton-Henry (1990, pp.16))

[44] Layton-Henry (1990, p.5).

[45] For example, the residence period required for permanent status is 5 years in Belgium and the Netherlands, 3 in France and 2 in Denmark. (Niessen (1989) in: Soysal (1994, p.121) in: Baldwin-Edwards (1997).)

in Austria, Germany and Switzerland.[46] [47]

It is apparent that in those countries where citizenship is relatively easy to obtain, foreign citizens also enjoy more political rights. A specific symbolic importance of national voting rights does therefore not seem to have much explanatory power.

Rath (in Layton-Henry (1990, pp.127)) compares the political rights of migrant workers in seven major West European democracies (Belgium, France, Great Britain, the Federal Republic of Germany, the Netherlands, Sweden and Switzerland) in order to identify causes for country-specific attitudes towards an extension of the franchise to non-citizens. Among the country characteristics that were found to have an influence on immigration policies are size, homogeneity, degree of federalism, the nature of the countries' electoral systems and their historical traditions, particular political arrangements, internal conflicts or consensus, the strength of particular political traditions and confidence in national security and identity.

Many of these factors refer in one way or another to the degree of homogeneity and consensus among the native population and suggest that the stronger inner consensus on public policy issues is, the more willing countries are to extend the franchise to foreign citizens. This complies with the findings in our political economy model on immigration and income redistribution in Chapter 3. First, however, we will empirically analyse the fiscal impact of immigrants in Austria in Chapter 2.

[46]For an analysis of naturalisation laws in Sweden, Germany, United Kingdom, France, the Netherlands, Belgium and Switzerland see de Rham in Layton-Henry (1990, pp.158).

[47]Required residence periods are 4 years in the UK, 8 years in Germany and 10 years in Austria and Switzerland. (Niessen (1989) in: Soysal (1994, p.121) in: Baldwin-Edwards (1997))

Chapter 2

The Fiscal Impact of Immigrants in Austria - A Generational Accounting Analysis

2.1 Introduction

In the discussion on the fiscal costs and benefits of immigration for the host country, the burden that immigrants allegedly pose on social welfare systems has featured most prominently. Lately, however, immigration has been proposed as a means to alleviate the fiscal burdens associated with aging populations. It has been recognised years ago that demographic trends in most developed countries will not allow sustaining their current pension and health systems and will pose serious burdens on their public finances. Attempts to estimate fiscal contributions of immigrants usually take a cross-sectional perspective.[1] For a

[1]See for example Simon (1984) for the U.S., Akbari (1989) for Canada, Ulrich (1992) for Germany and Gustaffson and Osterberg (2001) for Sweden.

meaningful evaluation of immigrants' fiscal impact, however, an inter-temporal analysis is necessary. Such a framework allows to incorporate changes in fiscal payments and benefits over time due to the aging of populations. In the following, we will apply the method of generational accounting in order to evaluate the fiscal impact of immigrants in Austria. The method has been developed by Auerbach et al. (1991, 1994) in order to provide an indicator for the amount of intergenerational redistribution implied by a given fiscal policy. At the same time, it enables to measure the 'true' level of public debt as opposed to conventional records of the budget deficit and public debt, which are only of limited significance in the light of future public spending and tax revenues that are set by current fiscal policy. In generational accounting, not only the tax receipts and public expenditures of a given fiscal year are considered, but also expected future public revenues and expenditures related to currently living as well as future generations. Fiscal sustainability prevails, if the so-called inter-temporal budget constraint is satisfied - that is, if current public debt does not exceed the present value of future revenues minus spending. The degree of intergenerational redistribution is measured by the generational accounts of the current newborn and the next, future generation, that is, the present value of their taxes paid less their benefits received over their lifetime. For previous applications of generational accounting on the estimation of immigrants' fiscal impacts see Auerbach and Oreopoulos (2000) and Smith and Edmonston (1997) for the U.S. and Bonin et al. (2000) for Germany. Storesletten (2000) has used a calibrated general equilibrium overlapping generations model to estimate the long-term fiscal impact of immigrants in Sweden. Findings generally are that the fiscal impact of immigration on the host country is positive, depending on the age and skill composition of immigrants.

The chapter is organised as follows: the next section gives an

A survey on the literature is given in Poschner (1996).

overview of the method of generational accounting. Section 2.3 gives an overview of the macroeconomic and fiscal background in Austria in the year 1998. Section 2.4 describes the demographic and fiscal micro-data underlying the derivation of generational accounts. Section 2.5 presents the results and the ensuing inter-temporal state of Austrian public finances in the base year. In Section 2.6, we focus on the fiscal contribution of immigrants and calculate the effects of various immigration policies on total public debt. Section 2.7 provides a review of related literature, and Section 2.8 concludes.

2.2 The methodology of generational accounting

The method of generational accounting was developed by Auerbach et al. (1991, 1992, 1994) as a response to the shortcomings of conventional periodical budget accounting that does not consider the long-term revenue and expenditure implications of present fiscal policy. While yearly budget accounts cannot provide an indicator of intergenerational redistribution due to fiscal policy, generational accounts can. In the following, we will give a brief description of the method employed, as it can be found in more detail for example in Bonin (2001), Kotlikoff (1993, 2001) and Raffelhüschen (1999b).

2.2.1 The government's inter-temporal budget constraint

At the core of generational accounting is the inter-temporal budget constraint of the government (e.g. the entire public sector), which requires that the present value of prospective net tax payments to the public sector, imposed on either living or future born agents, must be sufficient to finance the present value of aggregate net debt. It is expressed in terms of the generational accounts $N_{t,k}$ of current and future generations (in present value terms of a base year t):

$$B_t = \sum_{s=0}^{d} N_{t,t-s} + \sum_{s=1}^{\infty} N_{t,t+s} \tag{2.1}$$

On the left-hand side of (2.1), B_t denotes the base year stock of government's explicit net debt (financial liabilities minus the sum of financial assets). It represents the sum of real government deficits (or surpluses) in the past, mirroring the spending and revenue history of the public sector. On the right-hand side, $N_{t,k}$ represents the present value as of year t of net tax payments (taxes paid minus transfers received) made by all members of a generation born in year k over the remaining life cycle: for generations currently alive, $N_{t,k}$ denotes remaining lifetime net taxes, for generations not yet born, $N_{t,k}$ refers to lifetime net taxes, discounted to the current year t. d defines the maximum age.

In testing for generational balance, generational accounting empirically evaluates whether current fiscal policy is consistent with the inter-temporal budget constraint of the public sector. If it is not, the adjustment of fiscal parameters in the budget constraint becomes necessary, either now or in the future. In the case that adjustment is carried out via future net taxes only, generational accounts would increase for future generations, implying fiscal redistribution between generations.

2.2.2 Generational accounts

In short, the generational account of a certain gender and age (and nativity) cohort is just the sum of discounted net tax payments that an individual of this specific gender and age (and nativity) cohort faces over its remaining life-span. The method of generational accounting is strictly forward-looking in the way that for each age cohort alive it only computes the aggregate net tax burden of a representative cohort member from a present base period on over its remaining life-time. The aggregate remaining lifetime net tax payments of a cohort born in period k, denoted $N_{t,k}$, is defined as

$$N_{t,k} = \sum_{s=\kappa}^{k+d} T_{s,k} P_{s,k} (1+r)^{-(s-t)} \quad with\ \kappa = max(t,k). \tag{2.2}$$

For currently living cohorts born in year k with $t-d \leq k \leq t$, $\kappa = t$; for future cohorts born in year $k > t$, $\kappa = k$. $T_{s,k}$ stands for the projected average net tax payments to the government in year s paid by a representative member of the generation born in year k. $P_{s,k}$ is the population of cohort k alive at time s. r represents the supposedly constant pre-tax interest rate applied to discount future payments back to the base period. The computation of the generational accounts therefore requires a demographic projection, taking account of fertility, mortality and migration trends, as well as a projection of the age-specific net tax payments by cohort, $T_{s,k}$. In combining projected age profiles with the projected population structure, one derives the rest-of-life net tax burden of living generations.

For living generations born in year k, the generational accounts in the base year t are just the aggregate remaining lifetime net tax payments divided by the number of cohort members alive in the base year:

$$GA_{t,k} = \frac{N_{t,k}}{P_{t,k}}. \tag{2.3}$$

Aggregate per capita net tax payments $T_{s,k}$ are found by summing up single per capita tax and transfer payments:

$$T_{s,k} = \sum_{i} t^{i}_{s,k}, \tag{2.4}$$

where $t^i_{s,k}$ indicates the average tax or transfer of type i paid or received by a representative k-born individual in period $s \geq t$, hence of age $s-k$. By convention, $t^i > 0$ defines a tax payment from the private to the public sector, and $t^i < 0$ defines a transfer payment from the public to the private sector.

For future generations, age-specific taxes and transfers are computed by simply projecting fiscal profiles of the base period using a constant productivity growth rate.[2] Fiscal profiles become

$$t^i_{t+j,k} = (1+g)^j t^i_{t,k-j}. \tag{2.5}$$

Equation (2.5) assigns to each agent of age $t+j-k$ in year $t+j$ the tax and transfer payment observed for agents of the same age in year t, adjusted for gains in productivity.

The base year cross-section of age-specific tax and transfer payments per capita is generally determined in two steps. First, the tax and transfer payments $\tau^i_{t,k}$ of a representative member of each age cohort are estimated from micro-data. In a second step, to overcome data deficiencies on the micro level, the individual age-specific taxes and transfers, summed up over all cohorts and weighted by the respective cohort number, are re-evaluated proportionally to fit the observed macroeconomic tax or transfer aggregate T^i_t by the application of a proportional, non-age-specific adjustment factor θ^i:

$$\theta^i = \frac{T^i_t}{\sum_{k=t-d}^{t} \tau^i_{t,k} P_{t,k}}. \tag{2.6}$$

From there, we derive adjusted per capita tax and transfer payments $t^i_{t,k}$ in the following way:

$$t^i_{t,k} = \theta^i \tau^i_{t,k}. \tag{2.7}$$

[2]It is therefore assumed that base year fiscal policy is maintained. See Bonin (2001, pp.25) on further details regarding the assumption of constant economic growth.

2.2.3 Determining future generational accounts and assessing fiscal imbalance

Within the method of generational accounting, there are different ways to construct the generational accounts for future generations and to assess the intergenerational stance of fiscal policy. First, one can proceed using (2.5) above, assuming that future generational accounts are equal to the one of the generation born in the base year, corrected only by the economic growth factor, as shown in (2.8) for the generation born one year after the base year:

$$GA_{t+1,t+1} = GA_{t,t}(1+g). \tag{2.8}$$

Then, from the inter-temporal budget constraint, one computes the inter-temporal public liabilities IPL_t of the base year as the difference between current debt and the aggregate net tax payments of living and future generations:

$$IPL_t = B_t - \sum_{k=t-d}^{\infty} N_{t,k}. \tag{2.9}$$

Inter-temporal public liabilities entail a revision of initial fiscal policy at some point in time - if they are positive (negative), a rise (decline) in net taxes is necessary eventually. Only if inter-temporal public liabilities are zero, fiscal policy is sustainable, since it does not violate the inter-temporal budget constraint of the government. The required policy adjustment can be undertaken in various ways. The conventional approach is to assign the uncovered liabilities in their entirety to future generations. Aggregate future net taxes then equal the difference between given current debt and the aggregate net tax payments of living generations, in order to ensure that the budget constraint holds. The generational accounts for all future generations are derived under the proposition that the government distributes the aggregate financing need evenly across future generations, assuming that generational accounts stay identical except for income growth. Depending on the choice of the specific future fiscal policy that is to correct the fiscal imbalance, the adjustment can be undertaken via a change in any of the given tax or transfer parameters $t^i_{s,k}$. For example, the factor determining the proportional rate of adjustment that is to be applied to all net tax payments of future born generations in order to raise additional net revenue to the extent of the inter-temporal public liabilities is equal to

$$\mu = \frac{IPL_t}{\sum_{k=t+1}^{\infty} P_{k,k}\overline{N}_{k,k}(1+r)^{t-k}}, \tag{2.10}$$

with $\overline{N}_{k,k}$ representing the present value lifetime net tax payments of a representative individual born in period $k > t$. This way, we can derive the new generational accounts of future born generations that guarantee fiscal sustainability under current tax and transfer policies. Accordingly, we can choose $\overline{N}_{k,k}$ to contain the present value of lifetime taxes or transfers only, or specific categories of each, to determine the necessary rate of adjustment of the chosen tax or transfer categories. Alternatively, the uniform adjustment factor can be applied to the present value life cycle taxes and/or transfers of both living and future generations - in this case, it would be assumed that government immediately switches to a sustainable path of fiscal policy, adjusting base year tax and/or transfer levels once and for all. Now, the degree of inter-temporal fiscal imbalance can be measured by the resulting difference in lifetime net tax payments between base year and future-born individuals. Selecting the cohort born immediately after the base year as representative for future generations, a second indicator for inter-temporal fiscal imbalance is the relative change in generational accounts between the generation born in the base year and in the year after:

$$\pi = \frac{GA_{t+1,t+1}}{GA_{t,t}(1+g)}. \tag{2.11}$$

Alternatively, one could measure the absolute change in the lifetime net tax payments of agents born in period t and $t+1$ that satisfies the inter-temporal budget constraint of the government. Fiscal policy is sustainable only if the thus derived future generational accounts are equal to the (growth-adjusted) generational account of the current new-born, that is, if π is equal to 1.

2.2.4 Generational accounting and immigration

Taking separate account of natives and immigrants as two subpopulations requires certain changes to the equations introduced above. The inter-temporal budget constraint in (2.1) is extended to incorporate the net taxes of current and future immigrants:

$$B_t = \sum_{s=0}^{d}(N_{t,t-s} + F_{t,t-s}) + \sum_{s=1}^{\infty}(N_{t,t+s} + F_{t,t+s}). \qquad (2.12)$$

Foreign aggregate cohort net tax payments $F_{t,k}$ are derived in analogy to those of natives presented in (2.2) above:

$$F_{t,k} = \sum_{s=\kappa}^{k+d} T^{*}_{s,k} P^{*}_{s,k} (1+r)^{-(s-t)} \quad with\ \kappa = max(t,k). \qquad (2.13)$$

The evolution of the foreign population $P^{*}_{s,k}$ over time will reflect not only fertility and mortality of immigrants, but also additional immigration as well as out-migration of previous immigrants (net migration). Per capita net tax payments of foreigners $T^{*}_{s,k}$ will typically differ from those of natives due to different economic characteristics of immigrants. Analogously to (2.4), aggregate foreign net tax payments are the sum of individual age-specific cohort profiles $\tau^{i*}_{t,k}$, respectively. These are re-evaluated again according to macroeconomic data by using the adjustment parameter θ^i, so that, given N different subpopulations, the following restriction is fulfilled:

$$T_t^i = \sum_n \sum_{k=t-d}^{t} t_{t,k}^{i,n} P_{t,k}^n = \theta^i \sum_n \sum_{k=t-d}^{t} \tau_{t,k}^{i,n} P_{t,k}^n. \qquad (2.14)$$

Generational accounts of foreigners are determined analogously to those of natives in (2.3) above:

$$GA_{t,k}^* = \frac{F_{t,k}}{P_{t,k}^*}. \qquad (2.15)$$

The generational accounts obtained will give an unambiguous indication of the fiscal burdens and contributions of immigrants and natives of all age-groups - given current fiscal policy, current macroeconomic conditions, and current demographic characteristics of natives and immigrants.[3] Therefore, even if absolute numbers are to be interpreted with caution, the generational accounting exercise holds valuable information concerning the relative fiscal stance of immigrants and natives as well as of current and future generations. More importantly still, generational accounts can be obtained for any specified scenario deviating from the status quo - and will yield important information concerning its consequences for inter-temporal fiscal balance and fiscal incidence among generations and subpopulations. Generational accounting can thus be used as a method for determining the net fiscal impact not only of immigration as it is, but also changes in immigration policy like changes in immigration quota or the immigration mix (e.g. the educational status of the immigrant population). Inter-temporal fiscal (im)balance will be affected by immigration in essentially two ways: firstly, they will have a demographic effect in enlarging the population (and thus the tax

[3]Future changes in either of these parameters, such as a change in the educational characteristics of future immigrants, cannot be taken into account, unless they are deliberately examined in a simulation exercise, which gives a valid result in the sense of a 'what-would-be-if' case when compared to the basic scenario.

base) and in altering its age- (and possibly gender-) composition[4]; secondly, they will probably change the fiscal characteristics of age cohorts due to a representative immigrant having higher or lower tax and transfer payments than a representative native of the same age and gender.

2.2.5 Practical issues

The standard technique in generational accounting is to project the base year age-specific tax and transfer payments into the future assuming that the observed relative levels of taxes and transfers stay constant and that absolute levels only change due to a uniform growth rate adjustment. This way, changes in tax and transfer profiles due to changes in fiscal policy and variations in the relative fiscal position of age groups are ignored, as well as cohort effects in the cross-sectional relative fiscal profiles, e.g. of immigrants. Generational accounts therefore have to be read appropriately, namely, as merely reflecting the status quo of fiscal policy as well as macroeconomic conditions. They can thus be used as meaningful indicators for the current state of public finances and reveal the relative fiscal burdens of the current newborn and the future-born generations as well as those of different subpopulations. They cannot be used as a reliable forecast of the future, since inevitable uncertainties concerning the future cannot be excluded from the analysis. Further, the results of generational accounting exercises crucially depend on the inputs used, namely the projections of populations, per capita taxes, transfers and government purchases, as well as the initial value of government net debt. Computed generational accounts can only be as good as the underlying micro-data. Besides, it is assumed in general that taxes are born by those paying the taxes, while trans-

[4]The demographic characteristics of immigrants usually affect fiscal imbalance in a positive way, due to a favourable average working age of immigrants. For details on the demographic data see Section 2.4.1.

fer payments are allocated to those who directly receive them.[5] However, it is not uncommon for generational accounting studies to display a great variety in fiscal incidence assumptions, which considerably hampers comparability.[6] An additional certain arbitrariness is implied by assumptions regarding the discount rate and the productivity growth rate. Here, it is common to perform sensitivity analyses in order to test for how much results deviate with a change in the values used.[7]

2.3 The macroeconomic and fiscal situation in Austria in the base year 1998

Since for the computation of generational accounts, the pattern of public revenues and expenditures specific to the base year is projected into the future and thus assumed to stay constant, some knowledge about the macroeconomic and fiscal environment in that year is helpful for an interpretation of the results.[8] The macroeconomic situation in 1998 was, with a real growth rate of 3.3 percent, a rather favourable one. However, this was not reflected much on the labour market or on fiscal parameters such as tax revenues and social spending, as these effects are commonly lagging behind the development of the growth rate. The fiscal situation in that year was predominately determined by previous efforts to fulfil the Maastricht deficit criterion for participation in the European Economic and Monetary Union

[5]For specific incidence assumptions used in the present analysis see Section 2.4.2.

[6]Even in the studies collected by the European Commission (1999) for the purpose of mutual comparability, different approaches were used for the construction of tax and transfer profiles (see Bonin (2001, p.34)).

[7]See Section 2.5.3.

[8]Lehner (1999).

(EMU). In order to bring down the budget deficit from its 5.1 percent of GDP in 1995 to a level below 3 percent, fiscal consolidation packages were enacted in 1996 and 1997. As mentioned in Keuschnigg et al. (2000), they consisted to the larger part of a cut in expenditures such as salaries and employment of civil servants and general administration, unemployment benefits and early retirement pensions. To a lesser part, revenues were increased via the wage and personal income taxes, as well as corporate and interest income taxes, an energy tax and a variety of indirect taxes. In 1997, the deficit rate decreased to 1.9 percent, with another increase in 1998 to 2.4 percent. Public debt decreased from around 70 percent of GDP in 1995 to 64.9 percent in 1998.[9] In order to get a clearer picture of the composition of these aggregate budget figures, we will now have a closer look at the public expenditures and revenues in 1998.

Public expenditures decreased from 57.2 percent of GDP in 1995 to 53.9 percent in 1997 and increased to 54.2 percent in 1998.[10] While the share of transfers in GDP in 1998 decreased relative to the previous year, expenditures from the statutory pension insurance, the most substantial transfer category of all, increased by about 4.2 percent relative to 1997.[11] In the long run, it is indeed the expected stark increase in pension outlays, due to increasing life expectancy and decreasing fertility under the current pay-as-you-go pension scheme, which puts perhaps the most important strain on the public budget. While the pension reform of November 1997 reduced the generosity of early retirement pensions and tightened eligibility criteria, the measures were judged not to reach far enough.[12] Similarly, spending pressures are present in the health care system. They were addressed by cost-reducing measures in the 1996 and 1997 budgets, including measures to increase the revenues of the health funds and to bring hospital

[9]WIFO (2003).
[10]Statistik Austria (2001a,b).
[11]Lehner (1999).
[12]OECD (1999, p.47).

financing together under one institution for each federal state, to help rationalise decisions. There is evidence that the diagnostics-based reimbursement scheme that displaced the former per-diem reimbursement scheme helped to curb public outlays for the provision of health services to some extent. However, a large potential for cost-cutting in the health sector remained.[13] Finally, expenditure on interest payments increased by 5.2 percent in 1998, which was solely due to the increase in public debt, since the average interest rate on public debt decreased relative to 1997.[14]

As to the public revenues, the share of taxes in GDP increased significantly from 24.8 percent of GDP in 1997 to 25.6 percent in 1998. In particular, revenue from the corporate, income and labour tax increased, mainly due to the legislative measures taken in the 1996 tax reform package *(Strukturanpassungsgesetz 1996)* including the abolition of preferential tax treatments as well as an increase in tax pre-payments.[15]

Table 2.1 below shows the data for the consolidated budget in Austria in the base year 1998, as they were used for the benchmarking of aggregated micro-data. The macroeconomic data on revenues were taken from national accounts data in Statistik Austria (2001a) and data from the Association of Austrian Social Insurance Institutions *(Hauptverband der österreichischen Sozialversicherungsträger)* (1999). Aggregate data on expenditures were taken from the report on social expenditure by the Federal Ministry of Social Security and Generations (*Bundesministerium für soziale Sicherheit und Generationen)* (1999). As these aggregate data on public revenues and expenditures need to correspond to the respective microeconomic survey data, single budget items were regrouped and summed up as described in the next section below. Intergovernmental grants and transfers were cancelled out.[16] Thus, we derive aggregate revenues

[13] OECD (1999, p.48).
[14] Lehner (1999).
[15] Lehner (1999, p.370), OECD (1999, p.40).
[16] Compare Keuschnigg et al. (2000).

and expenditures of 1036.199 billion (bn.) ATS each. It can be seen that most of the revenue in that year was generated by social security contributions, followed by the value added tax and the labour income tax. On the expenditure side, government consumption and pensions were the biggest items, followed by education, interest payments and health expenditures.

Table 2.1: Consolidated budget in Austria (1998).

RECEIPTS		EXPENDITURES	
Personal income tax	44.124	Pensions	258.142
Labour income tax	201.979	Old age care	21.297
Social security contributions	397.498	Health	95.691
Capital income taxes	20.014	Unemployment	23.467
Value added tax	215.838	Family-related benefits	53.126
Other indirect taxes	92.446	Social assistance	3.721
Public deficit	64.300	Education grants	1.589
		Education	158.187
		Government consumption	322.479
		Interest payments	98.500
Total	1.036.199	Total	1.036.199

Note: In bn. ATS.

Source: BMSG (1999), Hauptverband der österreichischen Sozialversicherungsträger (1999), OENB (2000), Statistik Austria (2001a).

2.4 Empirical derivation of generational accounts

The construction of generational accounts for living and future generations requires data on current and future populations as well as net tax payments by cohorts. In the following, we will describe the data sources and assumptions used for 1) the population projections and 2) the disaggregating of the Austrian budget in 1998 into tax and transfer profiles according to age, sex and nativity. Along with the majority of other generational accounting studies[17], we group generations into 5-year age cohorts.[18] We have four subpopulations: native men, native women, foreign men and foreign women. The reason for choosing 1998 as the base year instead of a more recent year lies in the availability of the required data. More exactly, most of the micro-data on taxes and transfers by nativity are only available from the European Community Household Panel (ECHP), the most recent wave of which (1999)[19] is referring to labour and income tax data of the year 1998, as will be discussed in detail below.

2.4.1 Demographic scenarios

For the population data of living and future generations by age, sex and nativity, we refer to Statistik Austria population projections based on the latest population census from 2001.[20] While the projections of the population data are modelled explicitly by

[17]See for example Bonin (2001) and European Commission (1999).

[18]This aggregation does not represent too much of a distortion as long as there are no large single age groups within those cohorts that exhibit a distinctly different pattern of tax payments and transfer benefits. For example, an increase in the number of oldest old would make the exact distribution of net taxes among this population group more important (see Bonin (2001, p.108).

[19]At the time that the study was undertaken.

[20]Data were obtained from Gustav Lebhart, Statistik Austria.

age and sex, they do not account separately for natives and foreigners. Thus, in order to derive the required population projections for natives as well as foreigners, we resort to the assumption that the proportion of foreigners in Austria is constant and equal to their average population share during the three latest years available: 2000, 2001 and 2002.

Statistik Austria (2003a) gives an overview over historic as well as projected demographic developments on the basis of the latest population census in 2001, and highlights the related changes in the age composition of the Austrian population as well as their importance for economic and political decision-making. Birth rates in Austria have decreased since their increases during the years 1988-1993, when the baby-boom generations of the 1960s reached parental age. Since 1993, the Austrian population has been growing, yet at a decreasing rate. The fertility rate has declined from around 4 in 1900 to its historic low of 1.33 in 2001. On the other hand, life expectancy has nearly doubled, from 40.6 (1899/1902) to 75.8 (2002) for men and 43.4 (1899/1902) to 81.7 (2002) for women. At the end of 1999, the number of Austria's inhabitants first hit the 8 million mark; at the beginning of the year 2002, 8.04 million people lived in Austria. The larger part of this population growth is to be attributed to net migration, which has been positive since the beginning of the 1960s. The current proportion of Austria's foreign-born inhabitants is with nearly 12 percent at a historic high. The population projections used rely on the following assumptions regarding mortality, fertility and migration. The fertility rate is assumed to stay at a new long-term level of 1.4 from 2002 onwards. Life expectancy at birth is assumed to increase by 7.2 years for men and 6.3 years for women in 2002 to 83.0 and 88.0 in 2050, respectively, and to remain constant thereafter. 60-year-old men are expected to reach an average age of more than 85 after 2050, 60-year-old women an average age of more than 89. The decreasing number of births and the increasing number of deaths would lead to a decrease in the population from around 2050 by 0.5 percent per year without migration. Due to immigration, Austria's population is expected to increase from 8.05 million in 2002 to 8.43 million in 2027. Net immigration data have been corrected upwards since the last official forecast and are assumed to increase from 17300 in 2001 to around 29000 in 2006 due to the expansion of the European Union in 2004, but to decrease from then onwards to 22500 in 2050. From 2028 onwards, net immigration is expected to stay below the birth deficit and thus lead to a decrease in the total population that is to reach about 20000 people per year by 2050. In our sensitivity analysis in Section 5.3, we test for the effects of higher as well as lower net immigration and fertility on generational accounts and fiscal imbalance.

2.4.2 Fiscal scenarios

Next, we need to specify the age-, sex- and nativity-specific personal tax and transfer payments, the so-called cohort profiles. For this, as outlined in Section 2, for this, we first determine the base year per capita tax and transfer payments of the various age cohorts $(\tau^i_{t,t-d}, ..., \tau^i_{t,k}, ..., \tau^i_{t,t})$ in each of our subpopulations, distinguished by nativity and sex: native men, native women, foreign men and foreign women. The personal and household micro data used to construct the cohort profiles and the generational accounts presented in this study were mainly taken from survey data in the European Community Household Panel (ECHP), years 1998 and 1999. The ECHP provides a large sample consisting of about 60000 households with about 130000 individuals in Europe, which are surveyed through 15 years. In Austria, about 3000 households are participating, with about 7000 individuals. The data are available on the household as well as the individual level. Following Bonin (2001), we assign most individual tax and transfer data directly, in the year when the tax or transfer payment is reported to have occurred. Even though this incidence assumption may not always accurately reflect the actual fiscal benefits and burdens of an individual, we stick to it as a feasible second-best solution.[21] Fiscal data that are only available at the household level in the ECHP (that is, in our case, housing and social assistance benefits), are allocated to individuals by assuming that the total amount reported is distributed evenly among all household members. This assignment is also likely to be misrepresentative of the actual incidence of tax and transfer payments within the household - however, as before, it seems reasonable for payments depending on the socio-economic composition of households, which stay representative as long as household composition does not change. The ECHP survey data are complemented by micro data provided by the Austrian Statistical Office as well as the Upper Austrian Health Insurance Administration *(Gebietskrankenkasse Oberösterreich)*. In a second step, the age profiles are benchmarked against the respective overall public budget data as presented in Table 1 by application of the adjustment factor θ^i that was described in (2.6). Those data were then smoothed by building moving averages among cohort values. In doing so, we hope to ameliorate variances in the data that are due to small sample sizes and retain representative cohort profiles. In addition, we are enlarging the sample size by drawing on both the survey results of 1998 and 1999. We now turn to explain the data sources and specific assumptions employed for arriving at the individual cohort profiles for each of our tax and transfer categories.

Tax and contribution payments

Labour income tax data and social insurance contributions data are not available by nativity from national statistical sources. The *Lohnsteuerstatistik* published by Statistik Austria[22] does not account separately for native Austrians and immigrants. For the

[21] See Bonin (2001, pp.107) for possible flaws and a justification of this incidence approach.

[22] That was used for the first generational evaluation of Austrian public finances by Keuschnigg et al. (1998).

same reason, it was not possible to resort to data from the Association of Austrian Social Insurance Institutions for age-gender-nativity profiles of social security contributions. The ECHP's detailed data on gross and net labour income by age, gender and nativity were therefore used to estimate individual average wage taxes plus social security contributions.[23] Thus, payroll contributions to the state-organized, pay-as-you-go financed social insurance are regarded as an integral part of gross wages and are assigned fully to workers. Due to data limitations it was not possible to construct separate profiles for wage taxes on the one hand, and the different contributions to social security (that is, contributions to the public pension scheme, statutory health and accident insurance and unemployment insurance) on the other hand. Tax payments and social security contributions from the usual two-months extra pay that is not included in the gross and net income data were derived from given yearly gross income data by subjecting taxable additional income to the tax tariff applicable. Filed personal income taxes *(veranlagte Einkommensteuer)* were obtained directly from the ECHP, together with any reimbursements or additional payments in the following year, which were deducted or added to the income tax data to obtain the final values. From the social security contributions of the self-employed, only contributions to the public pension scheme are available directly. Contributions to the statutory health and accident insurance of the self-employed, not surveyed by the ECHP, are allocated along their contributions to pensions, since health insurance contributions are a fixed percentage of gross earnings as well, subject to the same contribution threshold. Contributions of pensioners to the statutory health scheme, which are strictly proportional to pension income, are assigned with the relative distribution of pension benefits by age,

[23]The fact that variables of the ECHP are not imputed, poses the problem of a bias due to missing values in cases where an answer was refused. However, because of the small frequency of such cases (a maximum of 11 percent of total), the bias is likely to be small.

sex and nativity.[24] Tax payments on pension income were calculated from given net pension income, by taking account of the income tax tariff and applicable deductions. The tax burden on private capital income, which is strictly proportional, is allocated according to the capital income profiles generated from the ECHP data on net of tax revenue from interest and dividends. Taxes on business like the corporate tax as well as other, minor taxes like the tax on business capital income are assumed to be borne by business capital and are not assigned to the household sector. This means that they are distributed uniformly among cohorts as part of the residual in public revenues that are not age-specific and therefore not allocated directly to individuals.[25] [26] Indirect tax payments (value-added tax and other indirect taxes) are not surveyed in the ECHP and had to be inferred from consumption expenditure data for adult equivalents[27] in the Statistik Austria's consumption survey *(Konsumerhebung)* 1999/2000 by 5-year age cohorts[28] of household heads and 12 consumption categories[29]. Separate tax profiles were computed for each consumption category, since the share of the different consumption goods in total purchases varies with age, and so do tax payments, therefore. The tax rates to be applied were computed as the means of tax rates applicable to the different

[24]So are pension insurance contributions by retired civil servants, due to the lack of a more appropriate assignment mechanism.

[25]See Garvey and Espenshade (1996) and Clune (1997). Alternatively, one could assign those taxes to private individuals according to their annual revenue from private capital income (compare Bonin (2001, p.109)). However, since it is difficult to determine the true incidence of such taxes, we go for the most general option.

[26]Similarly, no 'inflation tax' or minor taxes on private capital like the private wealth tax or the property tax are assigned to individuals according to their interest and dividend income (see Bonin (2001, pp.110)).

[27]Household expenditure adjusted according to the size and type of household.

[28]From 24 and younger to 75 and older.

[29]As listed in COICOP (Classification of the Individual Consumption Expenditures by Purpose).

consumption good COICOP subcategories[30] and can differ from the formal value-added tax rates of 10 percent and 20 percent on goods for basic needs and other goods, respectively, depending on the composition of consumption goods in the various categories. Except for one-person households, the consumption survey does not distinguish between household heads by sex, and male and female consumption tax payments therefore had to be assumed to be equal. Also, due to the lack in data, consumption patterns were not available separately for natives and foreigners. Therefore, foreign tax payments had to be distributed in proportion to the relative average consumption expenditure level of foreigners, assuming an identical consumption pattern of foreigners and natives. As with labour and capital income taxes and social security contributions, incidence is assumed to lie with the taxpayers, that is, in this case, the household heads. Dependent children are assumed not to bear any tax burden themselves.[31] Among other indirect taxes, some of the most important ones are the taxes on stimulants (mainly alcohol and tobacco) and beverages, excise duties on energy and mineral oil, the *Normverbrauchsabgabe (Nova)* and the insurance tax, which together make up about 89 percent of total revenue from other indirect taxes on goods and services.[32] These tax payments are distributed in proportion to the amount of average cohort expenditure subject to the respective tax.

---

[30]Provided by Bernhard Mazegger (Statistik Austria) on request.

[31]Data limitations in the consumption survey regarding the composition of households by age of household head prevents us from following a common procedure of distributing part of the indirect tax burden among infant household members by certain consumption weights. In the approach use, children are treated as a 'consumption good whose quality, which is related to their commodity consumption, enters the parents' utility function, but is a substitute for parents' own consumption of commodities' (Razin and Sadka (1995, p.14) in: Bonin (2001, p.111)). An advantage of this perspective is that both the level as well as the relative age distribution of consumption do not necessarily vary in line with fertility, and the assumption of constant tax profiles in the light of demographic change is justified (Bonin (2001, p.111)).

[32]Statistische Nachrichten (2001a, pp.875).

Transfer receipts

Expenditure profiles are also to a large part constructed by making use of the ECHP's detailed survey of benefit recipiency, which is, at the same time, the only source for determining transfers within Austria's social security system by nativity. Cohort-specific individual receipts of pension benefits, monetary health care benefits, unemployment benefits, family-related benefits, old-age care, social assistance and education grants are derived from the respective average transfer receipts of individuals in the ECHP. Cohort profiles for pension benefits include public pension income of all sorts - that is primarily old-age pensions, early retirement pensions, survivors' pensions and invalidity pensions. In the original cross-section, average pension receipts of natives decline with the age of pensioners, reflecting past differences in working careers. In order to avoid projecting this implausible lifetime pattern of pension payments into the future, we follow the procedure described in Bonin (2001, pp.112) and design maturation effects in the following way: for native male cohorts older than 70 and native female cohorts older than 80, we assume that average pension receipts in the initial cross-section remain constant over the remaining life cycle (apart from productivity growth). For younger base year cohorts and all future cohorts, we hold the received pension amount constant from the age of 70 (80), when average per capita pension receipts are at or close to the maximum in the base year. Profiles on health care benefits comprise monetary benefits derived from the ECHP as well as health care related in-kind benefits[33], which were available by 5-year age groups, sex and nativity from the Upper Austrian Health Insurance Administration[34] [35]. With family-related

[33]Comprising *Arztkosten, Krankenhauskosten, Medikamentenkosten, Heilbehelfe- und Hilfsmittelkosten, Fahrtspesen, Transportkosten.*

[34]Provided by Jürgen Himmelbauer (*Oberösterreichische Gebietskrankenkasse, Gesundheitsberichterstattung*) on request.

[35]The Upper Austrian data seem to represent the national data pretty well, as is revealed in a comparison with health care benefit profiles using

benefits[36], incidence is assumed not to lie with transfer recipients but with the children who are the cause for the transfer to take place. Allocating family-related benefits to those household members who are classified as dependent children justifies assuming that the initial profile of adults stays unchanged when fertility changes and, for example, the average number of children per household falls.[37] As in the case of family-related benefits, household (instead of individual) data are used for constructing age profiles for public housing support[38] and social assistance *(Sozialhilfe der Länder und Gemeinden in Form von Geldleistungen).* Here, too, transfer recipiency does not mainly depend on individual characteristics but on characteristics of the household. Therefore, in order to set up transfer profiles which are more likely to stay representative in the course of demographic transition, housing support and social assistance benefits are distributed evenly among all household members. Unemployment insurance benefits[39], emergency welfare benefits *(Notstandshilfe)*[40], old-age transfers[41] and education grants[42] again are derived from individual transfer receipts surveyed in the ECHP.

data on Austrian health care cost patterns ('acute health care costs' containing *Arzt-, Krankenhaus-, Medikamentekosten*) from Riedel and Hofmarcher (2001).

[36]Comprising *Familienbeihilfe, Wochengeld und Karenzgeld, Geburtenbeihilfe und sonstige Familienleistungen.*

[37]See Bonin (2001, p.116).

[38]Comprising *Wohnbeihilfe, Mietzinsbeihilfe, Mietbeihilfe vom Sozialamt, sonstige Wohnungsunterstützungen, Annuitätenzuschüsse.*

[39]*Arbeitslosengeld, Beihilfen aus der Arbeitsmarktverwaltung und Sonderunterstützung.*

[40]A specific welfare benefit for the unemployed who do not receive unemployment benefits any longer.

[41]Old-age transfers include payments received of any public institution and therefore take account of both the Austrian federal old-age care (*Bundespflegegeld aus der Pensions- und Unfallversicherung*) as well as the *Länder* transfers.

[42]*Unterstützung für Schul-/Berufsausbildung und/oder Studium, sonstige ausbildungsbezogene Unterstützungen.*

Finally, in-kind education expenditure[43] is assigned explicitly to the receiving age cohorts, since it also represents government expenditure that is dependent on age. Future education expenditure is assumed to develop proportionally to the fraction of an age cohort enrolled in the educational system. Per capita educational expenditure is again assumed to stay constant apart from productivity growth. In using Statistik Austria[44] educational expenditure data by school type[45] together with pre-school and school enrolment statistics[46], age profiles are constructed for pre-schools *(Krippen, Kindergärten, Horte)*, primary education, lower secondary education, higher secondary and vocational education and tertiary education (comprising universities, *Kunsthochschulen* and *Fachhochschulen*). The rest of net government expenditure, which does not display a specific age-gender-nativity pattern, is allocated lump sum to all cohorts.

In establishing age-gender-nativity profiles for the tax and transfer categories listed above, (the major part in) public revenues and expenditures are traced down with respect to individual characteristics of taxpayers and transfer recipients. The distribution of taxes and transfers that results from both legal regulations as well as individual economic circumstances is analysed. Age will doubtlessly make a difference, as well as gender - as for nativity, it is often claimed to be the case. Here, however, evidence from the exercise above will have to be examined in detail yet.

[43] *Personalaufwand, Sachaufwand und Investitionen.*

[44] Statistik Austria (2002).

[45] According to the International Standard Classification of Education 1997.

[46] Provided by Wolfgang Pauli (Statistik Austria, *Direktion Bevölkerung*) and Sabine Martinschitz (Statistik Austria, *Direktion Volkswirtschaft*) on request.

Tax payments and transfer receipts in the base year 1998

In order to ensure that aggregate per capita tax and transfer payments of cohorts correspond to their respective public sector budget values in the year surveyed, the micro data profiles described above are re-evaluated by the adjustment parameter described in (2.6). The public sector budget underlying the generational accounts is displayed in Table 1. Tax and transfer payments are included irrespective of the federal level of government, also including the parafiscal social insurance institutions, in order to reflect the public sector net payments of generations as comprehensively as possible. Reported government purchases were derived as the net value of the public sector receipts and expenditures that were taken account of, and reflect public spending that cannot be assigned reliably to specific age groups, such as government consumption of goods and services, public subsidies and public sector personnel spending. Figures 2.1, 2.2 and 2.3 below display the absolute per capita tax and transfer payments of representative cohort members in 1998 obtained by benchmarking the surveyed micro profiles against the base year budget.[47] As stated in Bonin (2001, p.121), it is the age pattern of absolute net tax burdens that is a major determinant for the sensitivity of public sector budgets to demographic influences. In Figure 2.1, we can see that the base year cross section of absolute tax payments of cohorts is dominated by the life cycle distribution of average wage income, owing to the fact that labour income taxes and social security contributions represent the major part in public revenues.[48] Tax payments are highest during working age, irrespective of gender and nativity, and peak at the age of 45 to 50 for native men and 40 to 45 for native women. They decline towards standard retirement age, when cases of unemployment

[47]Displayed values were also smoothed by calculating moving averages across age cohorts as described above.

[48]They accounted for about 60 percent of total public revenue in 1998 (OENB (2003)).

and early retirement increase. Average tax payments of women are smaller than those of men throughout their life and in total represent about 50 percent of aggregate male payments, due to a smaller average labour force participation as well as average income of women. During retirement age, indirect taxes gain weight in total tax payments, which are lower both for native males and females. Gender-specific differences among foreign tax profiles are similar, thought not quite as pronounced.

Figure 2.1: Cohort-specific tax payments. Cross section of the year 1998.

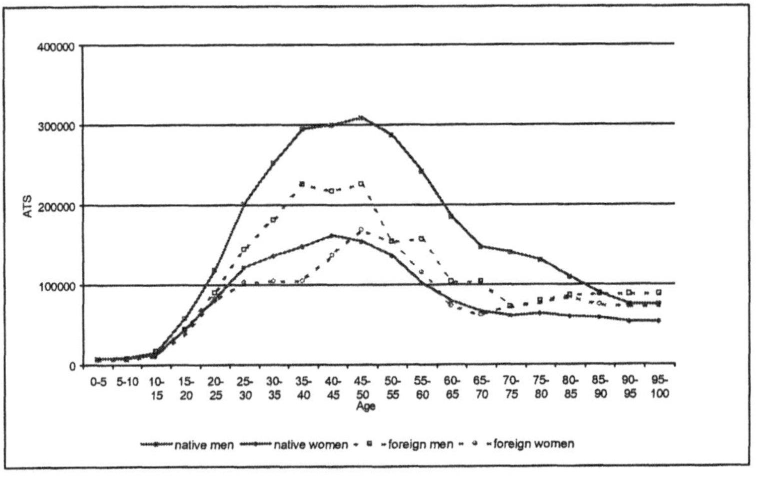

Among cross-sectional transfer receipts of cohorts, the largest share falls on pension, education and statutory health care benefits.[49] Educational and family-related transfers are dominating

[49]They accounted for about 50, 10 and 20 percent of total transfers in 1998, respectively (BMSG (1999)).

total transfer receipts until the age of 25 to 30 for all cohorts. At this age, differences in transfer receipts between males and females as well as natives and foreigners are negligible. For older persons, health care benefits dominate the absolute transfer pattern, until the age of 50 to 55, when pension benefits become the most important determinant of average transfers receipts. Male and female health transfers are fairly similar throughout the life-cycle, with women receiving higher transfers than men during child-bearing age and at very old age. For foreigners, the same pattern is observed, while total health outlays increase less markedly than those for natives from the age of 55 to 60, until they are only about 50 and 65 percent than those of native men and women among the oldest-old.[50] Gender-specific differences are especially apparent with pension benefits for both natives and foreigners, which reflect differences in income and thus pension contributions during working age. While total transfers decrease for native men older than 75 to 80 due to above mentioned maturation effects in pension transfers, they keep increasing for native women until the age of 90 mainly due to growing old-age care as well as health benefits.

Figure 2.3 below shows the cohort-specific net tax burdens in 1998, that is, their average annual tax payments less transfer receipts. We can see that while native men are net contributors to the public system during the age of 20 to 60, net tax payments of women are only positive during the age of 25 to 55, and they are smaller. In their youth as well as during retirement age, individuals are net beneficiaries from the public tax and transfer system. The pattern of foreign male and female net payments is similar to that of natives, though the absolute amount paid is smaller for a large part of the life-cycle, respectively, most distinctively so for men. Net payments of foreign women exceed those of native women from the age of 45. Also, they turn nega-

[50]For the cross-sectional distributions of the single tax and transfer categories see Figures 2.9-2.19 in Appendix 2.A.

Figure 2.2: Cohort-specific transfers. Cross section of the year 1998.

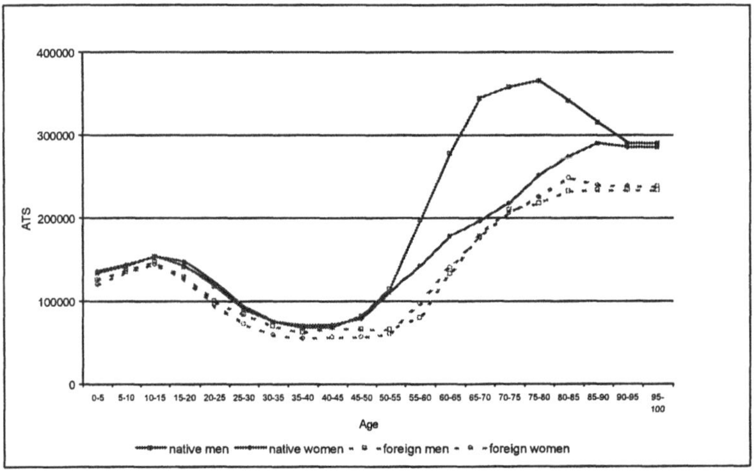

tive later in life for both foreign men and women in comparison to their native counterparts. As to the extent of redistribution between generations, genders and natives and foreigners, no final conclusions can be drawn from this cross-sectional survey. For a valid evaluation of absolute and relative net tax burdens of cohorts, we need to take demographic parameters, such as population size and mortality, into account. This is done within the generational accounting framework, which uses population projections to determine the present value of rest-of-life net tax payments of cohorts, while assuming that the base year amounts of revenue and spending stay constant except for productivity growth. For the long-term productivity growth rate, we use 1.5 percent in the base case scenario, in accordance with the generational accounting studies collected by the European Commission (1999). As discussed in Bonin (2001, pp.130), the discount rate used for calculating the present value of future payments in generational accounting studies usually ranges above the average rate of return on risk-free government bonds to incorporate the premium paid for risk, but below the return on private sector capital, which tends to be more volatile than public payments streams. We use a discount rate of 5 percent for the base case, again to render results comparable with European Commission (1999) studies. However, we will also carry out sensitivity tests in order to test for the effect that the assumption of a different discount rate has on our results. Thus, in Section 2.5.3 we compute generational accounts based on discount rates of four and six percent, assuming that risk aversion or uncertainty of future net tax payments is lower or higher than in the base case, respectively. The following section presents the calculated generational accounts for natives as well as foreigners in Austria in 1998 and analyses the according inter-temporal sustainability of Austrian public finances.

2.5 Generational redistribution in Austria

2.5.1 Generational accounts of present generations

In Figure 2.4, we see the gender- and nationality-specific generational accounts for generations living in the base year. Since generational accounts represent the present values of rest-of-life net tax payments of generations, they are not comparable across age groups. We can, however, still compare the intra-generational differences in net tax burdens between our fiscally distinct sub-

Figure 2.3: Cohort-specific net tax payments. Cross section of the year 1998.

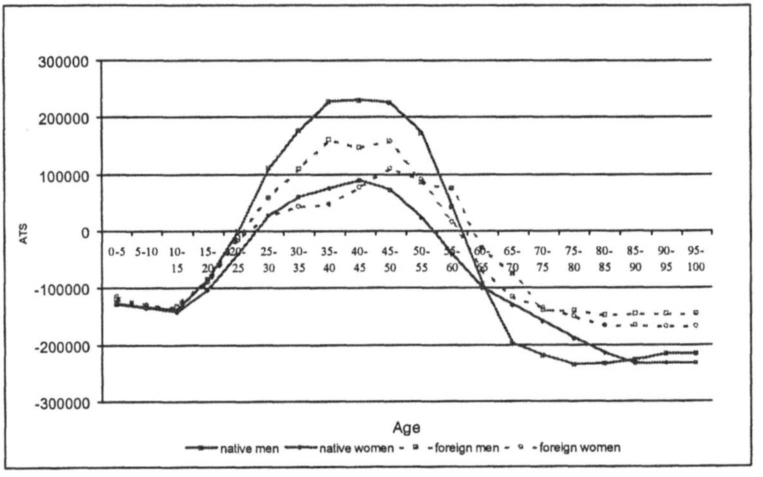

populations of native men, native women, foreign men and foreign women.

The generational accounts display the characteristic lifetime pattern of net tax payments independent of gender and nationality. During youth, rest-of-life net payments gradually increase because youth-specific transfers disappear and high tax payments during working age are discounted less and thus gain in weight. Among cohorts born in the year 1998, lifetime net taxes are negative and thus constitute net transfers. They are lowest for native men at a value of ATS 273600, followed by those for foreign men, foreign women and native women, who on average receive a present value of ATS 488700, ATS 1018600 and ATS 1840000 over their lifetimes, respectively. Rest-of-life net taxes

Figure 2.4: Generational accounts for living generations by gender and nationality. Base year 1998. Growth rate 1.5 percent, discount rate 5 percent.

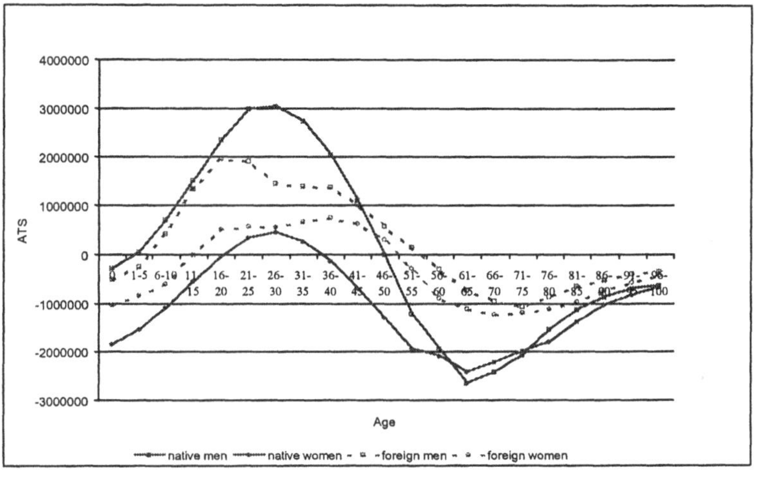

peak at the age of 26-30 (ATS 3044000), 16-20 (ATS 1969900), 36-40 (ATS 758800) and 26-30 (ATS 457200), respectively. At that point, the present value of rest-of-life net tax payments is highest due to high present tax payments versus transfers that, for the largest part, occur only later in life and still are heavily discounted. From then on, generational accounts fall continuously, since increases in annual tax payments due to rising average labour income, as displayed in Figure 2.1, are offset by the effects of an increasingly shorter working career and less discounted retirement transfers. The generational accounts of representative individuals turn negative beyond the age of 50 and 35 for native men and women, respectively, and beyond the age of 45 and 50 for foreign men and women, respectively. Rest-of-life net transfers peak at the age of 61-65 for native men (ATS 2637500) and women (ATS 2416800), and they are highest at the age of 71-75 for foreign men (ATS 1049900) and at the age of 66-70 for foreign women (ATS 1208700). Thereafter, remaining lifetime net benefits decline steadily, as a result of shorter life expectancy conditional on age. Gender-specific differences in rest-of-life net tax burdens are apparent both among natives and foreigners. Over the entire life cycle, native men are expected to receive by ATS 1566400 less in net transfers than native women. This discrepancy of male and female generational accounts increases to a maximum of ATS 2641100 that native men at the age of 21-25 on average are expected to pay more than native women of the same age over the rest of their lives. Unsurprisingly, this difference in generational accounts peaks after the age that individuals enter the labour force, when labour supply and probably labour income are likely to differ significantly between males and females of working age. Differences in gender-specific net tax burdens vanish for older base year generations. As transfer receipts during retirement age gain weight, the generational accounts of native male cohorts approach the value of those of female cohorts due to higher annual transfer receipts received by men (see Figure 2.2). From the age of 76, however, net transfers for native women exceed those for men yet again due to the effect of a higher life expectancy of women. Among foreigners, gender-specific differences in net tax burdens by age are similar, though not quite as pronounced. While over the entire lifecycle, foreign men are expected to pay ATS 529900 more in net taxes than foreign women, their additional net tax burden increases to a maximum of ATS 1451400 for cohorts of the age of 16-20. Differences in rest-of-life net tax burdens between foreign men and women decrease for older cohorts, but stay positive. As with natives, this points to considerable redistribution between the genders. If we compare generational accounts between natives and foreigners, we can see in Figure 2.5 that, generally, a representative native individual receives slightly more net transfers over the rest of his or her life than a representative foreign individual until the age of 20, and pays more in net taxes over the rest of his or her life during working age until the age of 35. For example, a native pays ATS 1758800 in rest-of-life net taxes at the age of 26-30, while a foreigner of the same age pays ATS 1032500 during the rest of his or her life. For cohorts older than 35, the picture looks different, and foreigners' rest-of-life net tax payments are higher than those of natives. This is explained by the fact that, on the one hand, foreign men and women become net transfer recipients later in life in comparison to native men and women, respectively, as can also be seen in Figure 2.3. On the other hand, net transfers to be received during the rest of their lives are significantly smaller in comparison to natives. The difference between native and foreign generational accounts peaks for cohorts of the age of 51-55. At that age, average rest-of-life net transfers of natives exceed those of foreigners by ATS 1571300.

Differences between the generational accounts of native men and foreign men are highest at the age of 61-65, when native men on average receive ATS 1918900 more than foreign men of the same age during the rest of their lives. The excess in rest-of-life net transfers of native women over those of foreign women is highest at the age of 51-55, at ATS 1648500. Interestingly, the rest-of-life net tax payments of foreign women exceed those of native women throughout the lifecycle. For men, this is only true for generations older than 45. The generational accounts of native men exceed those of foreign men during youth and working age. In total, net tax payments of currently living foreigners and natives are positive at ATS 538.5 billion and ATS 1346.9 billion, respectively. Aggregate net tax payments of current as well as future foreigners decrease to ATS 282.2 billion, while those of natives are negative at ATS -3064.0 billion, leaving foreigners as the only net contributors to the public budget.

Figure 2.5: Generational accounts for living generations by nationality. Base year 1998. Growth rate 1.5 percent, discount rate 5 percent.

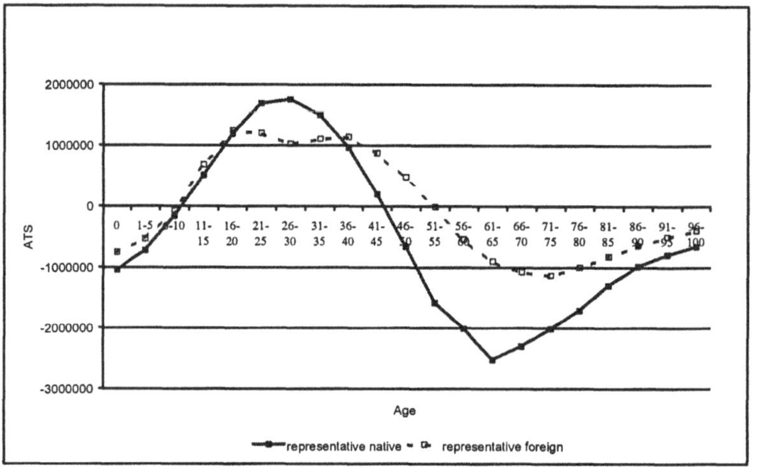

We can track the sources of nationality- and gender-specific redistribution by disaggregating the generational accounts into our various categories of taxes and transfers. Tables 2.13, 2.14, 2.15 and 2.16 in Appendix 2.B provide such a decomposition of generational accounts for native men, native women, foreign men and foreign women, respectively. In comparing Tables 2.13 and 2.14, we find, as expected, that differences in the generational accounts of native men and native women primarily come from higher labour income taxes and social security contributions of men. The present value of these payments during the life-time of base-year male newborns, for example, is almost 2.5 times that of female newborns. Gender differentials in rest-of-life labour taxes and social security contributions are highest for cohorts at or near their retirement age. Similarly, we find that native men pay higher capital income taxes, and receive higher pensions and unemployment benefits during the rest of their lives than native women. There are no significant differences as far as VAT and excise tax payments, health and family-related benefits, housing benefits, social assistance benefits or education are concerned. Here, in general, present values for female cohorts slightly exceed those for male cohorts - an exception are social assistance payments, which are higher for men until the age of 65, but fall below those for women for older cohorts. This is to be explained by higher social assistance payments to women among the oldest old on the one hand, and the higher life expectancy of women on the other. This effect is even more pronounced in the case of old-age care benefits, where women are expected to receive about two to three times the amount of men during the rest of their lives. In total, native men born in the base year are expected to receive about the same amount as women in transfers (ATS 2967000 versus ATS 2797000), whereas their expected tax payments are nearly two times higher (ATS 3769000 versus ATS 2078000)[51]. When looking at gender-specific differences in generational accounts among foreigners (Tables 2.15 and 2.16), we get similar results. Notable exceptions are old-age care benefits, which are higher for male than for female foreigners, and social assistance benefits, from which female foreigners benefit more than male foreigners over the rest of their lifetime. When comparing rest-of-life taxes and transfers between natives and foreigners, we notice that in most cohorts, natives pay higher rest-of-life taxes and also receive higher rest-of-life transfers in return. This effect is especially pronounced in the case of labour income taxes and social security contributions, as well as pension and old-age care benefits, but also health and housing benefits and, among men, social assistance benefits. One noteworthy ex-

[51]Adding up single rest-of-life tax payments and transfer receipts of newborns in Tables 2.13 and 2.14.

ception is unemployment benefits, where rest-of-life payments are higher for foreign men than native men up to the age of 35. For newborns in the base year, the value of expected tax payments for native men throughout their life is two times that for foreign men (ATS 3769000 versus ATS 1844000), whereas expected transfer benefits exceed those of foreign men to a slightly lesser extent (ATS 2967000 versus ATS 1573000). For female newborns, the respective values are similar, with ATS 2073000 versus ATS 1128000 of expected life-time tax payments, and ATS 2797000 versus ATS 1441000 of expected transfer benefits for native and foreign women, respectively.

Finally, one should remember that there are certain limitations for using absolute generational accounts for an interpretation of redistribution between natives and foreigners as well as genders.[52] As mentioned above, results are valid only given the underlying incidence assumptions. Thus, for example, generational accounts do not consider intra-household distribution. On the other hand, generational accounts do not say anything about redistribution relative to pre-tax resources. As shown in Bonin (2001), differences in fiscal burdens can appear considerably smaller when taking into account the life cycle income positions of subpopulations.

2.5.2 Inter-temporal fiscal imbalance

In order to determine the long-term fiscal sustainability of Austrian public finances in 1998, we compute the size of inter-temporal public liabilities, or the so-called 'true public debt', which is the difference between the nominal value of public debt at the beginning of the base year and aggregate present value net tax payments for living as well as future generations, extended out to infinity (see (2.9)). Therefore, we subtract from the officially recorded financial liabilities equal to 61.4 percent of the base year

[52]See Bonin (2001, p.137).

Table 2.2: The state of inter-temporal fiscal balance in Austria (1998).

IPL (% of GDP)		167.5
Official public debt (% of GDP)		61.4
Implicit government debt (% of GDP)		106.1
Percentage change required		
for future cohorts only:		
	all taxes and transfers	43.8
	taxes only	71.2
	transfers only	113.5
for all cohorts:		
	all taxes and transfers	8.2
	taxes only	14.4
	transfers only	18.9

GDP the sum of the generational accounts of all subpopulations, multiplied by the respective projected cohort sizes, which is equal to -106.1 percent of GDP. As a result, we obtain inter-temporal public liabilities amounting to 167.5 percent of GDP (see Table 2.2). This indicator is more accurate than common measures of fiscal soundness in that it comprises not only the official debt, but also future public liabilities and assets that are implied by present fiscal policy. The state of fiscal policy in Austria in 1998 was therefore unsustainable, since aggregate present and future expected net tax payments did not only not serve to cover existing debt, but were negative and thus expanded the gap in public finances even more.

In Tables 2.3 and 2.4, we see the difference between the age-specific and the non-age-specific[53] components of generational accounts, separately for natives and foreigners. Thus we derive

[53]Government purchases and the public deficit, which are distributed lump-sum to individuals. In both tables, the third column displays rest-of-

the generational accounts as the amounts to which cohort-specific rest-of-life per capita net government spending is not financed by respective net tax payments. Since government spending as well as the public deficit were distributed equally across age groups, the amount of rest-of-life net government spending per capita gradually declines with cohort age.[54] For a base year newborn native, age-specific rest-of-life net tax payments are positive, while they are negative for a base year newborn foreigner. Both, however, are exceeded by far by per capita rest-of-life net government purchases, which render generational accounts negative for natives as well as foreigners. When individuals get older, generational accounts rise due to rising present value net tax payments and declining rest-of-life government consumption. Per capita rest-of-life government consumption of foreigners is generally lower than that of natives due to a sharper decline in the foreign population towards old age. In addition, age-specific net payments of foreigners exceed those of natives at age 11-15 and from the age of 41 onwards. As a consequence, foreign generational accounts exceed those of natives from the age of 36 onwards. Since the present value of expected tax payments does not cover the present values of expected transfer payments and consumption spending, and, furthermore, the outstanding government debt of the base year needs to be redeemed, a policy adjustment is necessary.

This adjustment will entail either a rise in tax levels and/or a reduction in government spending levels, either for future generations only, or for both current and future generations, as de-

life per capita government purchases net of per capita shares in the public deficit, which constitutes an asset on the government's balance sheet (see Table 2.1).

[54]Exceptions are foreign cohorts aged 6-15, 36-40 and 51-60, which exhibit an increase in per capita rest-of-life net government spending compared to their preceding age cohorts. This effect is to be explained by projected cohort sizes.

Table 2.3: Age- and non-age-specific components of generational accounts for natives.[a,b]

Age	Age-specific net tax payments	Government consumption net of return on government assets	Generational account
0	58.5	1095.7	-1037.2
5	309.5	1031.3	-721.8
10	830.2	993.6	-163.4
15	1487.1	975.6	511.5
20	2156.6	962.9	1193.7
25	2648.0	951.5	1696.5
30	2615.1	856.2	1758.9
35	2299.4	798.2	1501.2
40	1720.6	756.4	964.1
45	930.9	731.7	199.2
50	13.5	672.1	-658.6
55	-952.5	626.5	-1579.0
60	-1492.4	512.1	-2004.5
65	-2032.7	487.7	-2520.5
70	-1908.9	390.1	-2299.1
75	-1689.2	321.9	-2011.1
80	-1444.3	262.9	-1707.2
85	-1105.1	191.4	-1296.5
90	-834.6	146.1	-980.7
95	-673.8	116.9	-790.6
100	-554.8	96.3	-651.1

[a] $r = 0.05$, $g = 0.015$.

[b] Thousands ATS (1998 present values).

scribed in Section 2.3.3. In Table 2.5, the effects of the various policy experiments on subpopulations' generational accounts are summed up. Let us assume, for a start, that future generations alone are to pay for the government's inter-temporal liabilities. In this case, a 71.2 percent increase in all future tax payments

Table 2.4: Age- and non-age-specific components of generational accounts for foreigners.[a,b]

Age	Age-specific net tax payments	Government consumption net of return on government assets	Generational account
0	-32.2	714.8	-747.0
5	180.2	711.6	-531.3
10	886.1	960.7	-74.6
15	1743.2	1055.7	687.5
20	2180.5	932.4	1248.1
25	1826.1	619.4	1206.8
30	1457.6	425.1	1032.5
35	1521.8	408.2	1113.6
40	1565.2	423.1	1142.1
45	1253.6	374.8	878.8
50	777.2	296.3	480.9
55	319.1	326.9	-7.8
60	-207.8	331.0	-538.8
65	-607.9	288.4	-896.3
70	-802.5	267.6	-1070.1
75	-880.0	246.8	-1126.8
80	-786.7	208.4	-995.1
85	-651.5	165.7	-817.3
90	-509.9	129.0	-638.9
95	-397.8	100.2	-498.0
100	-310.5	78.7	-389.2

[a] r = 0.05, g = 0.015.

[b] Thousands ATS (1998 present values).

or a 113.5 percent decrease of all future transfer payments (thus converting transfers into taxes, in fact) of future-born agents is required. If both tax and transfer payments are to be adjusted, a 43.8 percent tax increase and transfer decrease is sufficient. As a result, representative future-born agents face a growth-adjusted lifetime net tax payment of ATS 1489600 if they are native, or ATS 656600 if they are foreign. Since after this adjustment, the lifetime net payments of future native and foreign cohorts are positive, they can be used to redeem initial government debt plus net spending on living generations. In comparison to current newborns, future generations are now significantly worse off: the net tax burden of a representative native is higher by ATS 2526700, while that of a representative foreigner is higher by ATS 1403600. The indicator π, measuring the relative change in life-cycle net tax payments of present and future generations (see (1.11)), thus equals -1.44 for natives and -0.88 for foreigners. There is also additional intra-generational redistribution between the genders implied by such a uniform adjustment of future net tax payments: future born native males would face net payments of ATS 2631700 as compared to net transfers of ATS 273600 for 1998 born native males. Future native females, on the other hand, would face net taxes of ATS 290800, in comparison to the ATS 1840000 in net transfers received by native females born in the base year. Future-born foreign males have to pay ATS 1140800, in comparison to net benefits of ATS 488700 of their living peers; future-born foreign females pay ATS 143800, in comparison to ATS 1018600 received by base year new-borns. Now, we can also determine the proportional change in tax and/or transfer payments necessary to regain fiscal sustainability if applied to all generations, both currently living and future, from the base year onwards. This method of satisfying the inter-temporal budget constraint distributes the fiscal burden among a larger population and therefore relieves future generations, at the expense of currently living generations, who now have to face deterioration in their public accounts. In this case, for example, a permanent increase of all taxes by 14.45 percent[55] would be necessary to close the gap in public finances and equalise the

[55]Or a permanent decrease in all transfers by 18.89 percent, leading to a generational account of ATS -475100 and ATS -491800 for native and foreign newborns, respectively.

accounts of current and future newborns at positive net transfer levels of ATS 591600 (natives) and ATS 567900 (foreigners). The simultaneous attainment of fiscal sustainability and positive transfers to individuals is made possible by net tax payments of native men averaging ATS 274000 in the case of a tax adjustment. These payments serve to pay for existing debt as well as net transfers to native women, foreign men and foreign women, averaging ATS 1500200, ATS 220800 and ATS 935600 respectively, in case of a tax adjustment. It is evident that, with all of our three adjustment mechanisms[56], the absolute change in present value life-time net tax payments is highest for native men, followed by those of native women, foreign men and foreign women. After the adjustment, generational accounts of future new-born native females are higher than those of foreign females if it is either both taxes and transfers or transfers only that are adjusted for future generations.

These findings are roughly consistent with those of a previous analysis of Austrian public finances, based on the year 1995.[57] Results derived in this study under the same assumptions on the growth and discount rate are summarised in Table 2.6. When comparing total public debt values, for example, results indicate that fiscal sustainability has improved during 1995-1998, though a large gap of 167.5 percent of GDP still existed in 1998. Even if we take into account the fact that different microeconomic data sets[58] were used, we can cautiously draw the conclusion that the fiscal consolidation packages that were enacted in 1996 and 1997 are appearing here. Thus, we have evidence that these savings, which to a large part affected the amount and maturity of futu-

[56]Constant proportional adjustment of 1) all taxes and transfers, 2) all taxes only, or 3) all transfers only, applied to either future cohorts alone or all cohorts (currently living as well as future).

[57]Keuschnigg et al. (1999).

[58]Labour income taxes and social security contributions in the present study were derived from the ECHP instead of national statistical sources, education and health care benefits were derived from different sources, as well (see Section 2.4.2).

Table 2.5: Achieving inter-temporal fiscal balance.

	native	foreign	native male	native female	foreign male	foreign female
New generational account[a]						
for future cohorts only:						
all taxes and transfers	1489.6	656.6	2631.7	290.8	1140.8	143.8
taxes only	1046.0	379.6	2374.4	-348.2	935.7	-209.4
transfers only	2196.5	1098.1	3041.7	1309.4	1467.6	706.7
for all cohorts:						
all taxes and transfers	-541.1	-534.9	280.5	-1403.5	-205.4	-883.9
taxes only	-591.6	-567.9	274.0	-1500.2	-220.8	-935.6
transfers only	-475.1	-491.8	288.9	-1277.1	-185.3	-816.4
Increase in generational account required[a]						
for future cohorts only:						
all taxes and transfers	2526.7	1403.6	2905.3	2130.8	1629.5	1162.4
taxes only	2083.1	1126.6	2648.0	1491.8	1424.4	809.2
transfers only	3233.6	1845.1	3315.3	3149.4	1956.3	1725.3
for all cohorts:						
all taxes and transfers	1037.1	747.0	273.6	1840.0	488.7	1018.6
taxes only	3120.2	1873.6	2921.6	3331.8	1913.1	1827.8
transfers only	562.0	255.2	562.5	562.9	303.4	202.2
Status quo generational accounts	-1037.1	-747.0	-273.6	-1840.0	-488.7	-1018.6

[a] Thousands ATS (base year current values).

re pension benefits[59], were not only reflected in annual budget deficit data, but, to an even larger extent, in the more comprehensive indicator of inter-temporal public debt. As to the sources of inter-temporal fiscal imbalance, it is likely that the amount of existing debt as well as population aging play an important role. To look at the relative importance of these causes, we compute our fiscal imbalance indicators under the assumptions that either there is no explicit government debt or that there is no population aging, both of which are supposed to significantly improve inter-temporal fiscal balance. Without any debt accumulated in the past, inter-temporal public liabilities would decline to 106.1 percent of base-year GDP. This implies a reduced financing burden on future generations, which would have to bear a 45.1 percent increase in taxes or a 71.89 percent decrease in transfers only, if they were to cover the public liabilities on their own. If both current and future generations shared the financing burden, the necessary tax (transfer) adjustment would decline further to a 9.15 percent increase (11.96 percent decrease). We can determine the effect of population aging on fiscal sustainability by assuming constant base-year fertility and mortality as in the benchmark variant of the Statistik Austria (2003b) population projections[60]. As a result, total public liabilities decline by 35.81 percentage points to 143.03 percent of base-year GDP. A proportional tax increase in all taxes by 81.98 percent (13.72 percent) would render public finances sustainable, if applied to future generations (current and future generations). If transfers were to be adjusted, the necessary decrease would be 117.78 percent for future generations, or 17.91 percent for current as well as future generations. In this scenario, the per capita fiscal burden increases for future generations, if they are to cover the financing gap on their own, even though inter-temporal public liabilities decrease.[61] It is also common for generational accountants to

[59] See Keuschnigg et al. (2000).

[60] Preliminary results as of September 8, 2003.

[61] This is due to a smaller projected total population, which is only slightly

Table 2.6: Austrian inter-temporal fiscal imbalance in the base year 1995.

IPL (% of GDP)		192.5		
Official public debt (% of GDP)		49.8		
Implicit government debt (% of GDP)		142.7		
Percentage change				
for future cohorts only:				
	taxes only	82.7		
for all cohorts:				
	taxes only	16.6		
	transfers only	14.8		
New generational account		average	male	female
for future cohorts only:				
	taxes only	1573.9	2215.9	899.0
for all cohorts:				
	taxes only	127.9		
	transfers only	122.6		
Increase in generational account required		average	male	female
for future cohorts only:				
	taxes only	1808.6	2109.1	1493.5
for all cohorts:				
	taxes only	362.5		
	transfers only	357.2		
Status quo generational accounts		-234.6	106.8	-594.5

[a] Results that are missing in this table are not reported in the publication.
[b] Thousands ATS (1998 current values, corrected for real productivity growth).
Source: Keuschnigg et al. (1999), pp.155.

check for the effect of population aging on inter-temporal public finances by keeping the population structure of the base year constant.[62] In our case, this would lead to a significant decrease in inter-temporal liabilities down to 42.87 percent of base-year GDP, and an according decrease in the financing burden on current and future generations (see Table 2.7). Indeed, if it was not for the debt already accumulated in the base year, the government would even accumulate an inter-temporal surplus of 18.57 percent of GDP. Tablc 2.7 summarises the results of these different scenarios. It is evident that a constant population structure has the most favourable effect on public finances. However, since this is a rather unrealistic scenario, it might be more interesting to assume constant fertility and mortality rates instead. In this scenario, inter-temporal public liabilities are reduced by 24.47 percentage points, which is not much in comparison to the savings effect in the scenario with no explicit debt: here, total public debt is smaller by 61.4 percentage points than in the base case.

more than 70 percent of the base case projection from 2050 onwards.

[62]Such a scenario, however, typically implies implausible survival rates (see Bonin (2001), pp.150) and is added here only for the sake of completeness.

Table 2.7: Sources of inter-temporal fiscal imbalance.

	Status quo	No explicit debt	No population aging: Constant fertility and mortality	No population aging: base-year population
IPL (% of GDP)	167.5	106.1	143.0	42.9
Official public debt (% of GDP)	61.4	0	61.4	61.4
Implicit government debt (% of GDP)	106.1	106.1	81.6	-18.6
Percentage change				
for future cohorts only:				
all taxes and transfers	43.9	27.7	48.3	9.6
taxes only	71.4	45.1	82.0	15.9
transfers only	114.0	71.9	117.8	24.2
for all cohorts:				
all taxes and transfers	8.2	5.2	7.8	2.3
taxes only	14.4	9.2	13.7	3.8
transfers only	18.9	12.0	18.0	5.7

2.5.3 Sensitivity analysis

Results presented in the previous sections were derived under certain assumptions regarding the projected population, the interest rate and the growth rate. In order to test for the robustness of the findings against variations in these underlying parameters, we carry out sensitivity tests for each, varying only one parameter at a time, while maintaining the status quo setting for all other variables.

Base year choice

Apart from the parameters mentioned, the chosen base year also has an important influence on the degree of inter-temporal fiscal imbalance, since it is the fiscal parameters of that specific year, which are projected into the future indefinitely. A comparison of fiscal imbalance indicators with those derived in the only other analysis of Austrian public finances (see Table 2.6 above) shows that inter-temporal fiscal sustainability improved slightly during 1995-1998, if we assume comparability despite of differences in the micro-economic data sets used[63]. Apart from a more favourable projected population structure[64], this might have to do with the fiscal consolidation packages enacted by the Austrian government in 1996 and 1997[65], as well as improved macro-economic conditions (annual real economic growth accel-

[63]See footnote 58. In addition, unlike in Keuschnigg et al. (1999), we derive generational accounts for foreigners explicitly. Since foreign tax and transfer payments are lower on average than those of natives, fiscal indicators can be expected to deviate.

[64]Although in the present study, both fertility as well as mortality is assumed to be lower than in the study by Keuschnigg et al. (1999) and thus rather detrimental to inter-temporal fiscal balance, net immigration is assumed to be higher (compare Section 2.4.1).

[65]The measures resulted in a decrease in pension and health outlays, most notably (compare Table 2.1 and Table I in Keuschnigg et al. (2000)).

erated from 1.6 percent in 1995 to 3.9 percent in 1998[66]). A comparison of generational accounts derived for the two base years (see Figure 2.6 below) reveals an increase in the generational accounts of most age cohorts over time, most significantly for males of working age, but also for those of retirement age. Since, despite of the pick-up in real growth rates, unemployment even increased slightly during the period[67], labour income taxes are not likely to have increased due to an increase in the tax base. Instead, tax rates were raised as part of the consolidation package, together with reductions on tax allowances and deductions. Besides, eligibility criteria for unemployment benefits were tightened, and public pension transfers were cut, especially by limiting early retirement.[68] A comparison of generational accounts disaggregated into the single tax and transfer categories confirms that the largest increase occurred in per capita labour income taxes and social security contributions, while per capita pension, health and unemployment benefits decreased.

Demographic parameters

In order to test for the sensitivity of fiscal imbalance indicators with regard to the underlying demographic parameters, we conduct the generational accounting analysis for a high as well as a low fertility scenario, and for a high as well as a low migration scenario. Under the high fertility scenario, the fertility rate is assumed to reach 1.7 from 2015 onwards (versus a constant 1.4 in the base case). The low fertility scenario is based on a fertility rate of 1.1, which is to come into effect from 2015 onwards, as well. As to the different migration scenarios, annual net immigration is assumed to increase (decrease) by 10000 relative to base case scenario. Annual net immigration is therefore assumed

[66]Statistik Austria (2003b).

[67]From 3.9 percent in 1995 to 4.5 percent in 1998, according to Eurostat definition (Statistik Austria (2003c)).

[68]See Section 2.3.

Figure 2.6: Generational accounts for living generations for the base years 1995 and 1998. Growth rate 1.5 percent, discount rate 5 percent.

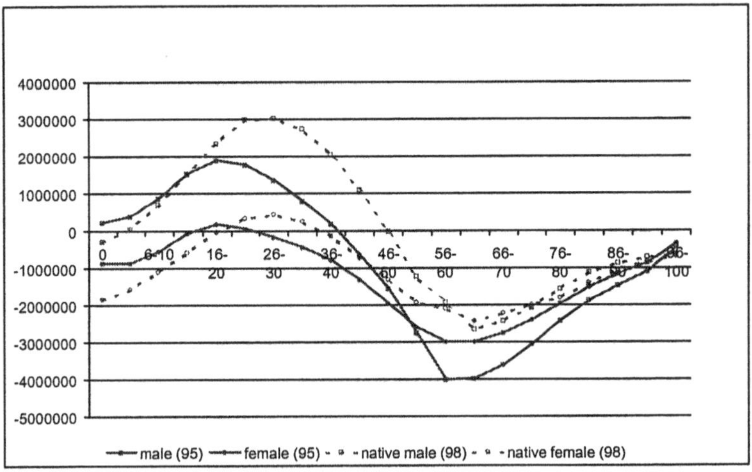

Note: 1998 current values. Values for the base year 1995 are from Keuschnigg et al. (1999) and are corrected for real productivity growth.

to fluctuate between 40000 (2006) and 30000 (2041) under the high migration scenario, and between 20000 (2006) and 10000 (2041) under the low migration scenario. Results of the various policy experiments are summed up in Table 2.8. It can be seen that higher (lower) fertility increases (decreases) inter-temporal fiscal imbalance. Since under base-year fiscal policy, newborns exhibit negative net tax payments over their lifetime, each additional newborn adds to the burden on the inter-temporal public budget. Likewise, the burden on future generations necessary to close the financing gap increases with fertility. While, for a given amount of total public debt, an increase in the cohort size of future generations would lead to a decrease in the per capita burden of future agents (the financing gap can now be distributed among a greater number of agents), the increase in total public debt outweighs this effect here.[69] If the financing gap is distributed both among current and future generations, we see that the respective additional financing need, measured by the lump-sum tax[70], increases as well, in comparison with the base case. Higher (lower) net immigration than in the base case results in slightly lower (higher) inter-temporal public liabilities. Since immigrants typically are of working age at the time of their entry into the country, they enlarge the group of net tax payers and thus reduce the inter-temporal fiscal burden. Compared to the specified changes in fertility, however, the effect of the specified changes in net immigration on inter-temporal fiscal balance is low. While, in our case, low (high) fertility leads to a decrease (increase) in total public debt by 17.1 (28.3) percentage points, high (low) migration reduces (raises) total public debt by only 3.7 (3.8) percentage points.

Growth and discount rate

The effects of varying growth and discount rate assumptions on fiscal imbalance indicators are displayed in Table 2.9. Changing the base case assumptions of long-term productivity growth

[69] In Bonin (2001), pp.153, increased fertility leads to a decrease in the burden on future agents necessary to close the sustainability gap.

[70] The lump-sum tax represents the annual additional average tax payment that each currently living and future individual has got to pay in order to balance the inter-temporal budget constraint. It is derived as the difference between the generational account of base year new-borns and their fictive generational account resulting from an application of the necessary percentage increase in net tax payments (not shown).

of 1.5 percent to 1 and 2 percent, and the discount rate of 5 percent to 2, 4 and 6 percent, can lead to an maximal increase (decrease) of inter-temporal public liabilities as a share of base year GDP by 184.0 (58.8) percentage points. Thereby, additional per capita net taxes levied on both current and future generations need to increase (decrease) by ATS 657200 (ATS 204100) in order to balance the inter-temporal budget constraint. Per capita net tax payments on members of future generations only are to increase (decrease) by ATS 1327600 (ATS 462400). It can be seen that total public debt increases with an increase in the growth rate, since negative base year net tax payments are magnified. It also increases with a decrease in the discount rate, since long-term cohort deficits due to population aging are given high weight. Accordingly, the additional tax burden on future as well as on current and future generations increases with lower discount and higher growth rates. The sensitivity analysis reveals that the generational account measures are robust at least qualitatively, even if the range of values obtained can be quite large, depending on the actual growth and discount rate values chosen. Even under the most optimistic scenario, assuming a growth rate of 1 percent and a discount rate of 6 percent, true public debt exceeds official public debt, expressed as a share of base year GDP, respectively, by 47.3 percentage points. This indicates that the continuation of current fiscal policy is likely to induce severe fiscal imbalances, and that fundamental policy changes are required.

Table 2.8: Sensitivity to demographic assumptions.

		Base case	High fertility	Low fertility	High migration	Low migration
IPL (% of GDP)		167.5	195.8	150.4	163.8	171.3
Generational account[a]						
	base year new-born	-1037.1	-1029.6	-1037.1	-994.2	-1080.7
	future new-born[b]	1489.6	1677.1	1441.5	1427.6	1558.4
Percentage change necessary						
for future cohorts only:						
	all taxes and transfers	43.8	47.2	42.9	40.6	47.3
	taxes only	71.2	78.8	67.9	65.6	77.6
	transfers only	113.5	117.7	116.6	106.5	121.1
for all cohorts:						
	all taxes and transfers	8.2	9.4	7.5	7.8	8.6
	taxes only	14.5	16.7	13.1	13.8	15.2
	transfers only	18.9	21.4	17.3	18.2	19.6
Lump-sum tax[a,c]		496.0	559.0	455.4	490.6	501.4

[a] Thousands ATS (base year current values).

[b] In order to render fiscal policy sustainable inter-temporally.

[c] See footnote 70 below.

Note: Generational accounts for natives. Base year 1998. Growth rate 1.5 percent, discount rate 5 percent.

Table 2.9: Sensitivity to growth and discount rate assumptions.

	Discount rate 4 percent	5 percent	6 percent
Growth rate: 1 percent			
IPL (% of GDP)	203.1	140.8	108.7
Generational account[a]			
base year new-born	-1052.6	-1043.2	-1076.9
future new-born[b]	1775.6	1280.0	1027.2
Lump-sum tax[a,c]	618.4	400.9	291.9
Growth rate: 1.5 percent			
IPL (% of GDP)	260.1	167.5	123.1
Generational account[a]			
base year new-born	-1112.5	-1037.1	-1058.1
future new-born[b]	2188.5	1489.6	1131.2
Lump-sum tax[a,c]	822.8	496.0	343.9
Growth rate: 2 percent			
IPL (% of GDP)	351.5	205.9	142.6
Generational account[a]			
base year new-born	-1250.6	-1054.6	-1042.3
future new-born[b]	2817.2	1780.9	1282.2
Lump-sum tax[a,c]	1153.2	632.5	413.3

[a] Thousands ATS (base year current values).
[b] In order to render fiscal policy sustainable inter-temporally.
[c] Annual additional average tax payment per capita of native population balancing the inter-temporal budget constraint.

Note: Generational accounts for natives. Base year 1998. Base case fertility, mortality and immigration.

2.6 Immigration policy and fiscal sustainability

Immigration is proposed frequently as a means to improve inter-temporal fiscal sustainability[71], because, on the one hand, immigrants typically augment the population share of individuals of working age, who are net contributors to the public budget. This effect is of particular importance in the light of the ongoing demographic aging of native populations. As discussed briefly in Section 2.4.1, the status quo migration scenario assumes annual net immigration to increase from 17300 in 2001 to around 29000 in 2006, and to decrease from then onwards to 22500 in 2050. Due to a lack in age-specific population projections for immigrants, net immigration is assumed to occur in such a way as to keep the population shares of foreigners in the various age groups constant to the average value of the years 2000-2002 from 2001 onwards. Thus, the favourable age composition of foreigners in these years, with more than 10 percent of age 25 to 35 and less than 0.5 percent of age 75 to 100 is assumed to persist in the future.[72] Figure 2.7 displays the average age composition of foreigners and natives in the years 2000-2002.[73] On the other hand, immigrants alleviate the burden on natives also for a given value of inter-temporal public debt, namely by increasing the number of agents who may share the additional net tax payments required in order to redeem the debt. Consequently, immigration might improve inter-temporal generational imbalance even if immigrant cohorts accumulate generational deficits.

[71]See for example Bonin (2001).

[72]A comparison of the foreign age composition in the year 1981 to the average of the years 2000-2002 shows that the age pattern persisted by and large; the relative share of foreigners among the oldest old even decreased.

[73]Author's calculations based on Statistik Austria data.

Figure 2.7: Age structure of foreigners and natives (2000-2002).

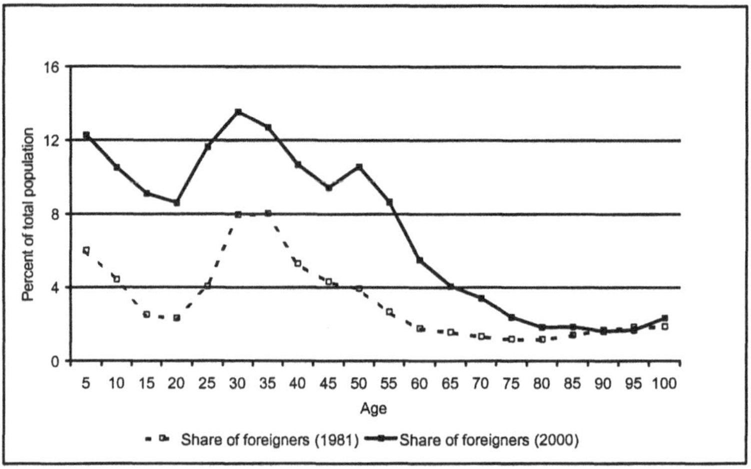

2.6.1 The fiscal contribution of immigrants

In the generational accounting exercise presented above, the fiscal characteristics of foreigners were derived explicitly, in order to distinguish the fiscal contributions of immigrants from those of natives within an inter-temporal setting. We estimated cross-sectional net tax payments of foreign cohorts as described in Section 2.4.2, and derived their generational accounts presented in Section 2.5.1 by assuming that the fiscal position of future immigrants equals that of residents of foreign origin of the same age and sex in the base year, corrected for productivity growth (compare equation (1.5)). As could be seen in Figures 2.4 and 2.5, foreigners in general pay smaller net tax payments and also receive smaller net transfer payments over their lifetime in return.[74] Tables 2.3 and 2.4 disaggregated native and foreign generational accounts into age- and non-age specific components. It could be seen that, unlike natives, newborn foreigners pose a burden on the inter-temporal public budget, even when abstracting from their share in government net spending. The maximum present value aggregate net payment is measured for immigrants entering the country close to age 20. Applying the age contribution of foreigners living in Austria in the base year, each immigrant contributes a net amount of approximately ATS 305000 on average throughout the rest of his or her life. Net contributions gradually decline for older immigrants, but remain positive for all agents younger than 50 when taking residency. Thus, if the net tax payments of future immigrants are indeed similar to those of current foreign residents, the foreign generational accounts indicate that immigrants who are of age 11 to 50 are most beneficial to the native population. Their lifetime net tax payments are positive and thus directly reduce the public financing gap. In the base year 1998, 84 percent of all immigrants belonged to those age cohorts with an estimated positive effect on inter-temporal public finances. Accordingly, if the current age distribution of immigrants stays unchanged in the future, immigration will contribute to the inter-temporal sustainability of public finances.

So far, we have assumed that immigration raises government consumption proportionately. As an alternative, we can separate government expenditure on public goods from total government consumption and assign the respective value on a per capita basis to natives only. This way, immigration does affect the amount of the public goods spending of government. In this case, we expect foreign generational accounts to improve and native generational accounts to worsen, as can be verified by comparing Tables 2.10 and 2.11, where public goods expenditure[75] is distributed to natives only, with Tables 2.3 and 2.4, where government consump-

[74]For further details, see Section 2.5.

[75]About 10 percent of non-age specific government expenditure, repre-

Table 2.10: Age- and non-age-specific components of generational accounts for natives.[a,b]

Age	Age-specific net tax payments	Government consumption net of return on government assets	Generational account
0	58.5	1117.8	-1059.3
5	309.5	1052.2	-742.7
10	830.2	1013.7	-183.5
15	1487.1	995.3	491.8
20	2156.6	982.4	1174.2
25	2648.0	970.8	1677.2
30	2615.1	873.5	1741.6
35	2299.4	814.3	1485.1
40	1720.6	771.6	948.9
45	930.9	746.5	184.4
50	13.5	685.7	-672.2
55	-952.5	639.2	-1591.7
60	-1492.4	522.4	-2014.8
65	-2032.7	497.5	-2530.3
70	-1908.9	398.0	-2307.0
75	-1689.2	328.4	-2017.6
80	-1444.3	268.2	-1712.5
85	-1105.1	195.3	-1300.4
90	-834.6	149.1	-983.7
95	-673.8	119.3	-793.0
100	-554.8	98.3	-653.1

[a] $r = 0.05$, $g = 0.015$.
[b] Thousands ATS (1998 present values).
Note: Expenditure on public goods accounted for separately.

tion was distributed lump-sum among total population.

senting the share of expenditure on national defence and judicial and foreign policy institutions in 1998 (BMF, 2004).

Table 2.11: Age- and non-age-specific components of generational accounts for foreigners.[a,b]

Age	Age-specific net tax payments	Government consumption net of return on government assets	Generational account
0	-32.2	618.3	-650.5
5	180.2	615.6	-435.3
10	886.1	831.0	55.1
15	1743.2	913.1	830.1
20	2180.5	806.5	1374.0
25	1826.1	535.8	1290.4
30	1457.6	367.7	1089.9
35	1521.8	353.1	1168.7
40	1565.2	366.0	1199.2
45	1253.6	324.2	929.4
50	777.2	256.3	520.9
55	319.1	282.8	36.3
60	-207.8	286.3	-494.1
65	-607.9	249.5	-857.4
70	-802.5	231.5	-1034.0
75	-880.0	213.5	-1093.5
80	-786.7	180.3	-967.0
85	-651.5	143.3	-794.9
90	-509.9	111.6	-621.5
95	-397.8	86.6	-484.4
100	-310.5	68.1	-378.6

[a] r = 0.05, g = 0.015.
[b] Thousands ATS (1998 present values).
Note: Expenditure on public goods accounted for separately.

The sustainability impacts of immigration policies

In the following, we will deal with the question of the extent to which future immigration may alleviate the inter-temporal fiscal burden on the native population in Austria. For this purpose, we compute the previously specified indicators of inter-temporal fiscal imbalance for different migration scenarios. As could be seen in Table 2.8, higher (lower) immigration than in the base case scenario lowers (raises) the inter-temporal public financing gap. This was to be expected, given the assumption of the constant favourable age distribution of foreigners. Since a representative immigrant to Austria is a net contributor to public finances under status quo conditions, each additional immigrant improves the inter-temporal sustainability of base year tax and transfer levels further.[76] We can also simulate the effect of immigration policies that actively screen immigrants for characteristics that are expected to improve their labour market performance and thus their potential for fiscal contribution. Following Bonin (2001), we assess the effect of immigration policies that select immigrants by skill and age on inter-temporal fiscal imbalance. First, we assume that by screening immigrants by skill, immigration policy effectively raises foreign base year net tax payments to the levels observed for natives.[77] In this case, as is shown in Table 2.12, inter-temporal fiscal liabilities decrease considerably, from 167.5 percent of base year GDP down to 151.68 percent. This is the case even though foreigners now not only exhibit higher present value net tax payments during working age, but also higher present value net transfer receipts during retirement age (see Figure 2.8).

[76]Still, a considerable financing gap remained even under the high immigration scenario, indicating that by immigration alone it will not be possible to achieve long-term fiscal sustainability.

[77]We can regard this scenario as an upper bound of the impact of screening by skill (compare Bonin (2001), p.186)).

Table 2.12: Screening of immigrants and inter-temporal fiscal imbalance.

		base case	screening	
			by skill	by age
IPL (% of GDP)		167.5	151.7	166.6
Generational account[a]				
	base year new-born	-1037.1	-1037.1	-1037.1
	future new-born[b]	1489.6	1218.1	1476.3
Percentage change necessary				
for future cohorts only:				
	all taxes and transfers	43.8	39.0	43.5
	taxes only	71.2	63.0	70.8
	transfers only	113.5	102.6	113.2
for all cohorts:				
	all taxes and transfers	8.2	7.3	8.2
	taxes only	14.5	12.8	14.4
	transfers only	18.9	16.9	18.8
Lump-sum tax[a]		496.0	444.7	493.8

[a] Thousands ATS (base year current values).
[b] In order to render fiscal policy sustainable inter-temporally.

Note: Generational accounts for natives. Base year 1998. Growth rate 1.5 percent, discount rate 5 percent.

Figure 2.8: Generational accounts of foreigners under immigration policies of screening. Growth rate 1.5 percent, discount rate 5 percent.

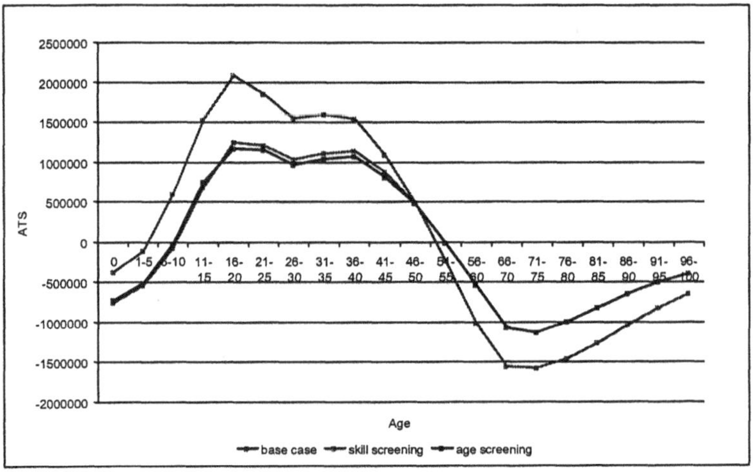

A representative foreigner now pays ATS 841610, which is more than twice the average foreign contribution in the base scenario.[78] As a result, the life-time net tax payments of future-born natives that are necessary to render public finances sustainable decrease by ATS 271500. If applied to both currently living and future generations, the necessary lump-sum tax on natives decreases by ATS 51330. Secondly, we assume that potential immigrants are screened by age and that, as a consequence, the fraction of male immigrants aged between 16 and 30 and female immigrants aged between 31 and 45 (females) who exhibit the highest cohort surpluses permanently increases by 20 percent while the absolute

[78]Not shown in the Table.

immigrant inflow stays unchanged.[79] In this case, inter-temporal fiscal imbalance is reduced slightly, with the tax burden on future generations falling by only ATS 13300, while those on both current and future generations falls by only ATS 2200. We can therefore conclude that for an immigration policy that intends to benefit public finances, screening by skill may be better suited than screening by age, due to the already favourable age composition of foreigners in Austria.[80]

2.7 Related literature

The first generational accounting analysis of Austrian public finances was done for the year 1995 by Keuschnigg et al. (1999, 2000) in the course of a round of studies based on a uniform method, which was initiated by the European Commission in 1998.[81] In comparison, the present generational accounting survey with 1998 as its base year provides an opportunity to assess the effects that fiscal policy measures and macroeconomic changes since 1995 had on Austrian generational accounts and the true public debt. However, it has to be said that direct comparability is limited due to inevitable differences in the microeconomic data sources used, and that one should therefore be cautious in the interpretation of results. Besides, the major aim here was to undertake a study that had not yet been done for Austria: namely, to compute generational accounts separately for natives and foreigners. This approach does not only allow to assess intergenerational but also intragenerational redistribution between natives and foreigners and also promises to contribute an answer to the often raised question about the extent to which immigration can be a solution to impending fiscal

[79]The immigrant share of all other age cohorts is reduced proportionately (compare Bonin (2001), p.187).

[80]Compare Bonin (2001) for a similar result.

[81]See Keuschnigg et al. (1999).

and, in particular, pension sustainability problems. Using generational accounting, Auerbach and Oreopoulos (1999) find that new immigrants reduce the fiscal burden borne by natives if the entire fiscal imbalance is placed on future generations. When the fiscal burden is shared by both current and future generations, whether there is a fiscal gain from immigration depends on the extent to which government purchases rise with the immigrant population. The impact of immigration on fiscal balance is found to be very small relative to the size of the overall imbalance itself. Smith and Edmonston (1997) contains another detailed evaluation of the future fiscal impact of immigrants in the US along the lines of the generational accounting method. It distinguishes immigrants not only by age, but also by educational level, immigrant generation and time since arrival, and estimate separate fiscal profiles for each of those immigrant categories. In addition, it computes immigrants' fiscal impact by level of government, i.e. the local, state and federal level. It is found that immigrants contribute positively on the federal level, because the positive effect of their relatively (in comparison to natives) favourable age distribution more than offsets the negative effect of their relatively lower education. The impact on the state and local level, however, is found to be negative, because the benefits (education, in particular) are received earlier in life than those on the federal level (pensions, health care) and are thus less heavily discounted. The total fiscal impact is positive for the average U.S. resident. Finally, Bonin, Raffelhüschen and Walliser (2000) used generational accounting to assess the fiscal impact of immigrants in Germany. They find the impact to be significantly positive if immigrants resemble current migrant residents in their economic characteristics. It is nevertheless too small to remove inter-temporal fiscal imbalance.

2.8 Conclusion

In this chapter, we employed generational accounting to analyse the inter-temporal stance of Austrian public finance in 1998 as well as the inter-temporal fiscal impact of immigration to Austria. Immigrants affect inter-temporal fiscal balance in essentially two ways. Firstly, they have a demographic effect in enlarging the population (and thus the tax base) and in altering its age- (and gender-) composition. Secondly, they change the fiscal characteristics of age cohorts due to a representative immigrant exhibiting higher or lower tax and transfer payments than a representative native of the same age and gender. The overall fiscal effect of immigration was found positive, under the assumption that the age and fiscal characteristics of future immigrants resemble those of the current immigrant population in Austria. This is due to a favourable age composition and lower per capita net transfer receipts during retirement age, which compensates for lower per capita net tax payments during working age. However, immigration is not likely to achieve inter-temporal fiscal balance, even if immigration increases or migrants are screened by skill or age.

2.A Tax payments and transfer receipts in 1998.

Figure 2.9: Labour income taxes and social security contributions.

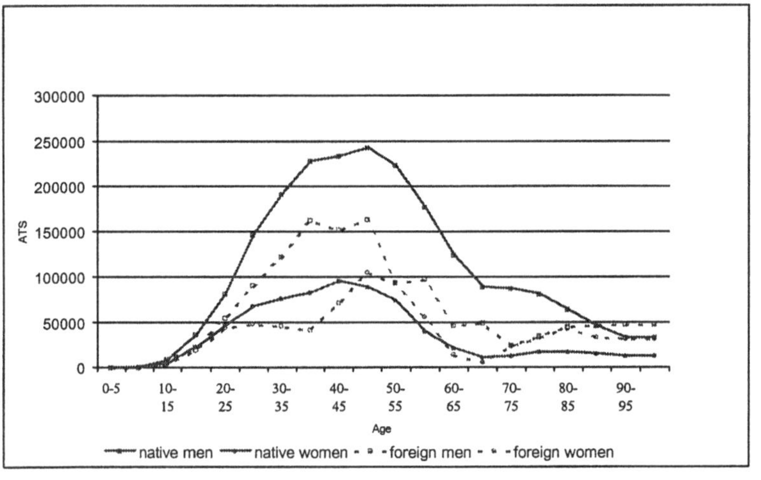

Figure 2.10: Capital income tax.

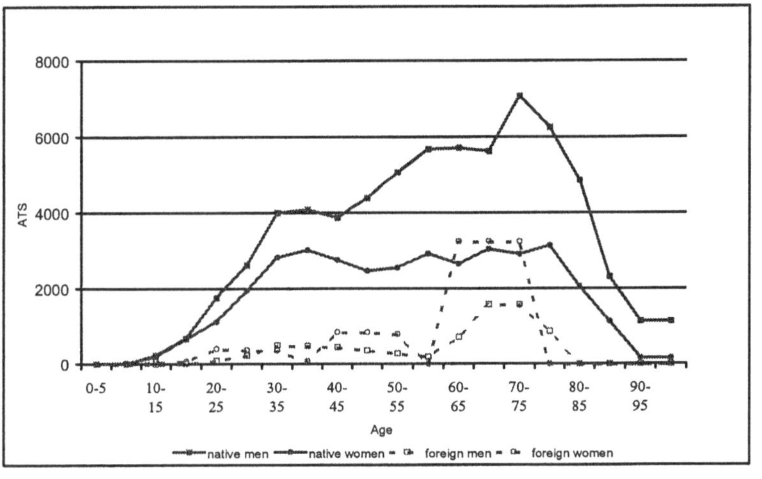

Figure 2.11: Value added tax and other indirect taxes.

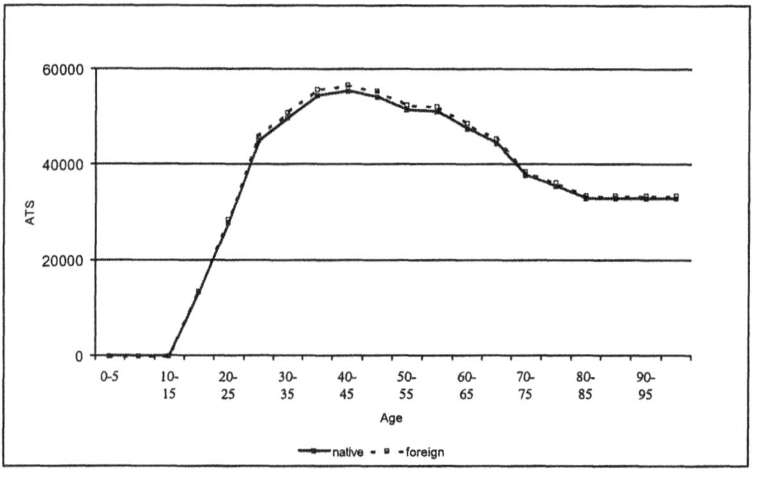

Figure 2.12: Pension transfers.

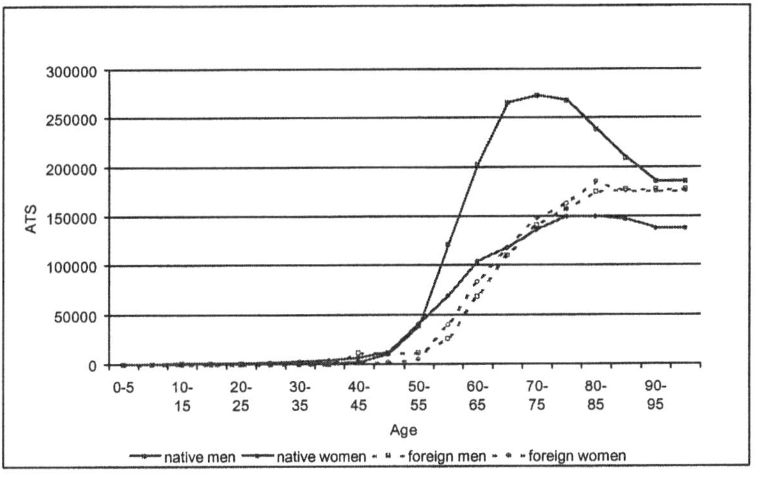

Figure 2.13: Health transfers.

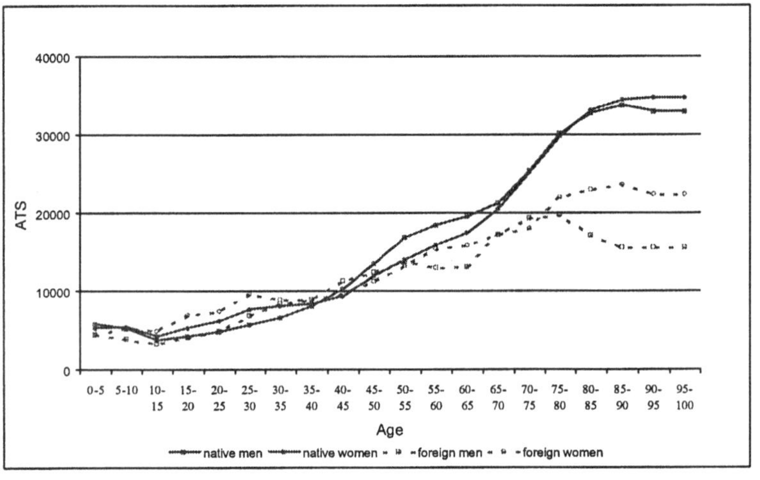

Figure 2.14: Family-related transfers.

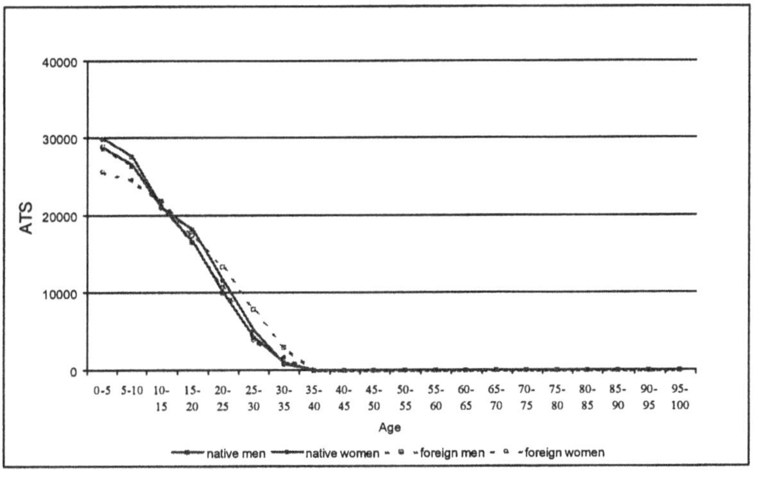

Figure 2.15: Housing transfers.

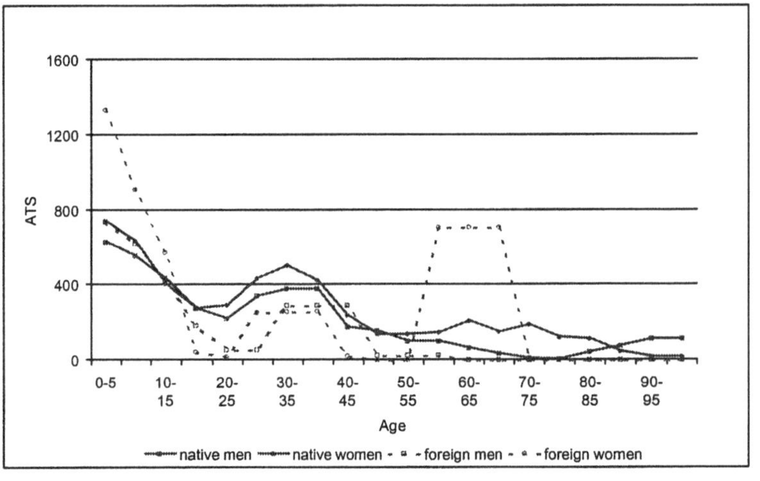

Figure 2.16: Old-age transfer.

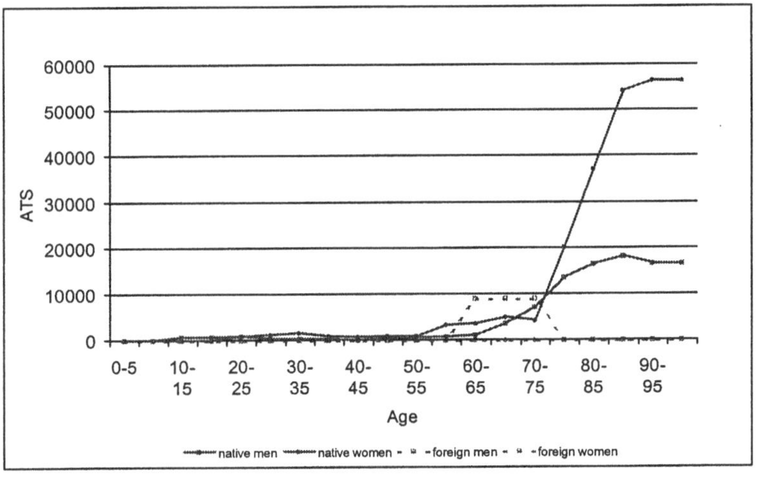

Figure 2.17: Unemployment transfer.

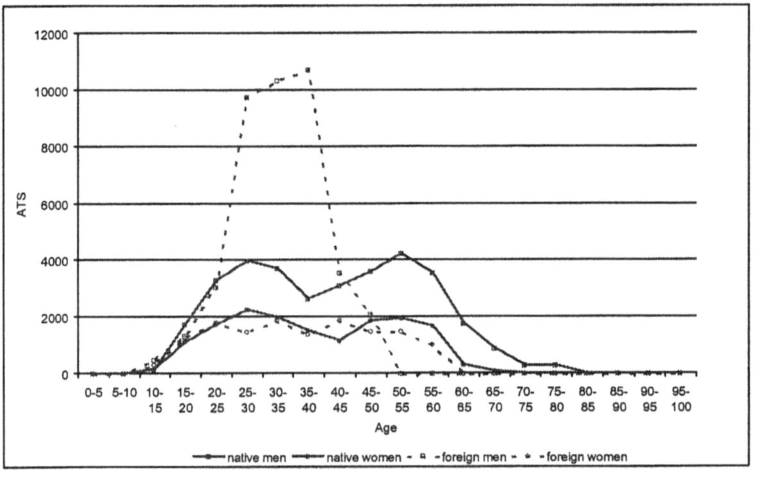

Figure 2.18: Social assistance.

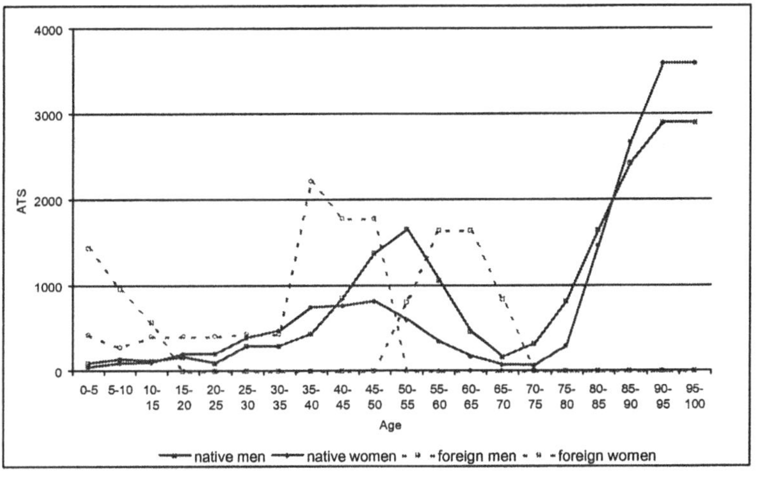

Figure 2.19: Educational transfers.

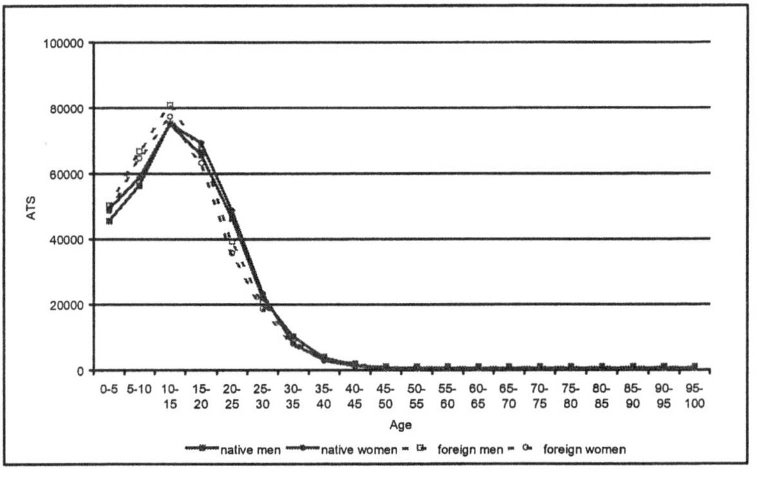

2.B The composition of generational accounts.

Table 2.13: The composition of generational accounts for native men.[a,b]

Generation's age in 1998	Generational account[c]	Tax payments: Labour income taxes and social security contributions	Tax payments: Capital income taxes	Tax payments: VAT/ excise taxes	Transfer receipts: Pensions	Transfer receipts: Health	Transfer receipts: Family-related benefits	Transfer receipts: Housing	Transfer receipts: Old age care	Transfer receipts: Unemployment	Transfer receipts: Social assistance	Transfer receipts: Education
0	-273.6	2890.1	69.0	809.8	918.1	281.3	457.5	12.1	30.7	56.6	12.4	1198.1
5	55.8	2955.4	70.1	826.7	905.9	268.4	385.9	10.6	30.8	58.2	12.3	1111.7
10	709.7	3332.7	78.7	931.3	999.2	270.6	280.7	8.8	34.2	65.7	13.3	989.9
15	1528.7	3875.6	91.4	1087.4	1168.8	289.9	186.3	7.4	38.6	76.3	14.8	791.7
20	2350.8	4416.1	104.6	1239.4	1373.4	317.4	109.9	6.6	42.1	84.5	16.6	525.6
25	2996.3	4902.4	117.0	1353.9	1606.7	348.3	51.0	6.3	45.3	86.6	18.7	293.6
30	3044.0	4768.9	115.0	1287.1	1659.9	343.5	16.5	5.6	42.8	76.2	19.1	133.6
35	2745.6	4608.3	114.8	1226.6	1864.4	358.5	3.0	4.5	46.0	67.0	20.2	60.4
40	2055.9	4234.0	111.3	1143.5	2159.8	377.1	0.0	3.2	51.9	59.9	21.6	27.5
45	1113.0	3820.9	112.3	1074.0	2621.5	406.7	0.0	2.1	62.0	56.8	22.9	16.7
50	1.9	3158.5	108.5	949.1	3006.9	408.7	0.0	1.6	69.5	48.5	20.8	13.0
55	-1216.4	2460.6	104.0	838.5	3477.7	404.3	0.0	1.1	79.1	36.7	16.4	11.8
60	-1924.0	1642.3	85.5	648.8	3357.1	345.1	0.0	0.7	79.7	20.5	10.5	9.4
65	-2637.5	1256.4	81.0	572.9	3618.1	350.0	0.0	0.5	101.8	10.0	8.8	8.8
70	-2411.0	873.8	64.2	418.4	2993.0	297.2	0.0	0.3	106.2	4.1	8.1	6.9
75	-2064.2	681.0	52.0	324.8	2421.6	272.8	0.0	0.2	116.8	1.6	9.7	5.7
80	-1531.6	480.8	34.8	249.4	1696.1	234.6	0.0	0.3	114.5	0.8	11.2	4.6
85	-1113.8	286.0	18.2	179.0	1134.6	180.4	0.0	0.3	93.0	0.0	11.5	3.4
90	-860.2	173.7	7.8	139.1	816.5	141.2	0.0	0.4	74.0	0.0	11.0	2.6
95	-695.7	114.9	3.9	112.9	635.8	113.0	0.0	0.4	56.5	0.0	9.9	2.1
100	-621.8	102.7	3.5	100.9	568.2	101.0	0.0	0.3	50.5	0.0	8.9	1.9

[a] r = 0.05, g = 0.015.
[b] Thousands ATS (1998 present values).
[c] Per capita shares in public deficit and government consumption included.

Table 2.14: The composition of generational accounts for native women.[a,b]

		Tax payments			Transfer receipts							
Generation's age in 1998	Generational account[c]	Labour income taxes and social security contributions	Capital income taxes	VAT/ excise taxes	Pensions	Health	Family-related benefits	Housing	Old age care	Unemployment	Social assistance	Education
0	-1840.0	1165.4	45.7	862.3	644.9	310.6	459.7	14.5	74.5	30.3	11.2	1251.1
5	-1537.6	1195.3	46.5	878.3	636.9	299.1	390.1	12.7	73.8	31.2	11.3	1151.6
10	-1083.7	1357.8	52.5	994.1	707.8	308.0	292.3	10.6	82.1	35.5	12.4	1021.5
15	-552.3	1563.1	60.4	1152.4	822.0	329.4	202.0	9.3	95.4	40.6	13.9	815.4
20	-26.6	1765.1	68.8	1321.5	972.2	361.4	125.2	8.9	113.3	44.4	15.6	546.7
25	355.2	1890.7	75.8	1440.3	1123.8	389.3	59.1	8.8	128.3	44.5	17.1	296.9
30	457.2	1749.2	73.2	1357.4	1142.6	371.9	17.9	7.7	121.5	38.1	16.4	123.8
35	264.9	1585.6	69.7	1269.3	1244.5	370.5	2.2	6.2	124.5	31.4	16.0	48.1
40	-126.0	1425.5	65.7	1204.0	1441.0	389.2	0.0	4.7	139.8	27.0	15.6	22.9
45	-687.3	1215.0	62.3	1135.2	1704.8	417.9	0.0	3.7	163.0	24.6	14.5	14.1
50	-1290.4	896.3	57.5	1009.6	1907.3	423.0	0.0	3.2	178.7	20.7	12.3	10.8
55	-1923.8	604.1	55.2	915.7	2161.3	435.3	0.0	3.1	205.6	14.2	10.3	10.1
60	-2080.3	345.1	45.7	725.5	2032.8	388.5	0.0	2.6	205.4	6.3	8.3	8.2
65	-2416.8	250.0	43.1	651.6	2167.2	408.6	0.0	2.4	244.1	1.2	8.9	7.8
70	-2207.2	189.1	34.3	493.8	1872.9	363.1	0.0	1.8	249.5	0.2	9.0	6.3
75	-1979.8	165.4	25.7	372.0	1594.0	319.6	0.0	1.3	274.1	0.0	10.2	5.1
80	-1793.1	142.4	17.8	292.7	1354.8	280.4	0.0	0.8	316.3	0.0	13.0	4.1
85	-1372.4	97.7	8.4	204.8	959.7	211.2	0.0	0.4	295.7	0.0	14.5	3.0
90	-1023.1	67.3	3.2	154.6	659.9	162.3	0.0	0.2	259.1	0.0	14.5	2.2
95	-817.0	47.3	0.6	122.5	514.1	129.2	0.0	0.1	209.9	0.0	13.4	1.8
100	-658.7	38.1	0.5	98.8	414.5	104.2	0.0	0.1	169.3	0.0	10.8	1.4

[a] r = 0.05, g = 0.015.
[b] Thousands ATS (1998 present values).
[c] Per capita shares in public deficit and government consumption included.

Table 2.15: The composition of generational accounts for foreign men.[a,b]

		Tax payments			Transfer receipts							
Generation's age in 1998	Generational account[c]	Labour income taxes and social security contributions	Capital income taxes	VAT/ excise taxes	Pensions	Health	Family-related benefits	Housing	Old age care	Unemployment	Social assistance	Education
0	-488.7	1257.9	39.9	545.7	111.3	149.0	341.2	8.0	4.3	68.4	12.5	877.9
5	-237.4	1399.5	44.1	606.4	119.8	153.2	304.2	7.0	4.6	76.5	10.0	850.7
10	425.2	2308.2	72.4	999.4	193.8	223.5	316.2	6.9	7.4	126.5	8.1	1029.5
15	1352.1	2983.2	94.1	1299.8	253.0	268.4	260.7	5.6	9.7	163.4	5.7	897.0
20	1969.9	3045.4	98.1	1331.3	267.2	263.0	171.9	4.3	10.2	166.3	4.3	562.8
25	1932.1	2481.9	82.7	1068.5	230.0	208.6	82.3	3.2	8.8	135.3	3.7	252.9
30	1462.1	1717.4	59.5	721.1	171.1	143.5	28.1	2.3	6.6	89.5	2.8	94.1
35	1408.8	1601.0	56.8	650.1	193.6	136.9	7.3	2.2	7.5	65.5	3.2	42.3
40	1388.2	1618.1	56.6	666.4	271.3	151.3	0.0	1.7	10.5	42.7	4.5	23.6
45	1039.0	1315.3	49.5	582.3	317.9	144.9	0.0	0.9	12.8	15.4	5.5	14.2
50	586.3	881.7	39.5	439.4	311.3	118.5	0.0	0.2	14.5	5.1	6.3	9.2
55	157.4	690.7	51.8	452.9	512.7	134.4	0.0	0.1	28.1	0.0	10.1	9.9
60	-296.1	565.8	74.0	440.5	791.6	143.8	0.0	0.1	50.1	0.0	10.7	10.2
65	-718.6	365.1	92.6	366.7	970.3	140.7	0.0	0.0	61.5	0.0	6.6	9.1
70	-936.6	305.8	93.6	314.0	1110.6	144.7	0.0	0.0	46.5	0.0	2.2	8.5
75	-1049.9	260.0	62.8	270.1	1177.7	138.9	0.0	0.0	23.5	0.0	0.0	8.0
80	-855.3	247.5	22.3	207.9	1007.7	107.7	0.0	0.0	0.0	0.0	0.0	6.4
85	-647.7	206.5	0.0	149.2	783.5	73.2	0.0	0.0	0.0	0.0	0.0	4.8
90	-509.6	167.8	0.0	118.0	624.4	55.1	0.0	0.0	0.0	0.0	0.0	3.8
95	-390.6	128.6	0.0	90.4	478.5	42.2	0.0	0.0	0.0	0.0	0.0	2.9
100	-340.4	112.1	0.0	78.8	417.0	36.8	0.0	0.0	0.0	0.0	0.0	2.5

[a] r = 0.05, g = 0.015.

[b] Thousands ATS (1998 present values).

[c] Per capita shares in public deficit and government consumption included.

Table 2.16: The composition of generational accounts for foreign women.[a,b]

Generation's age in 1998	Generational account[c]	Tax payments: Labour income taxes and social security contributions	Tax payments: Capital income taxes	Tax payments: VAT/ excise taxes	Transfer receipts: Pensions	Transfer receipts: Health	Transfer receipts: Family-related benefits	Transfer receipts: Housing	Transfer receipts: Old age care	Transfer receipts: Unemployment	Transfer receipts: Social assistance	Transfer receipts: Education
0	-1018.6	610.2	5.9	511.7	88.4	165.2	304.2	12.0	0.0	19.2	12.6	839.3
5	-839.2	678.4	6.6	568.1	94.1	171.6	271.2	9.7	0.0	21.5	12.9	810.3
10	-596.9	1117.2	10.7	935.3	151.1	250.3	279.5	8.2	0.0	35.4	18.8	973.9
15	-5.4	1439.4	13.8	1213.0	196.7	293.5	223.2	6.1	0.0	45.1	22.4	851.1
20	518.5	1408.4	13.6	1200.2	201.1	270.2	135.2	4.5	0.0	42.3	20.8	532.1
25	590.4	936.9	9.3	815.9	147.0	173.6	49.7	3.2	0.0	26.0	13.9	209.1
30	574.5	724.9	7.4	652.1	137.3	134.6	15.1	2.7	0.0	18.7	11.9	85.0
35	686.9	833.3	9.3	724.6	208.8	151.5	4.6	2.7	0.0	19.5	15.9	42.2
40	758.8	987.4	12.4	778.3	316.2	174.8	0.0	2.5	0.0	19.1	17.8	24.1
45	633.9	949.3	13.5	673.3	381.0	167.6	0.0	2.1	0.0	15.8	11.5	14.3
50	309.1	723.3	12.1	528.4	443.6	150.5	0.0	2.5	0.0	10.4	4.8	9.7
55	-275.3	556.5	16.6	568.0	825.5	190.3	0.0	4.9	0.0	7.7	0.0	11.0
60	-884.7	319.1	22.5	529.0	1164.5	200.9	0.0	6.0	0.0	3.0	0.0	10.8
65	-1109.0	176.0	24.2	412.1	1222.9	176.7	0.0	4.1	0.0	0.0	0.0	9.0
70	-1208.7	202.9	17.8	347.1	1310.8	173.1	0.0	1.9	0.0	0.0	0.0	8.2
75	-1185.8	254.3	8.3	286.2	1306.2	167.7	0.0	0.0	0.0	0.0	0.0	7.4
80	-1096.5	254.1	0.0	239.4	1205.6	157.1	0.0	0.0	0.0	0.0	0.0	6.4
85	-952.6	218.9	0.0	194.1	1041.5	134.0	0.0	0.0	0.0	0.0	0.0	5.4
90	-724.5	146.2	0.0	147.3	772.4	101.4	0.0	0.0	0.0	0.0	0.0	4.1
95	-567.4	110.2	0.0	115.0	603.0	76.9	0.0	0.0	0.0	0.0	0.0	3.2
100	-420.4	81.6	0.0	85.2	446.8	57.0	0.0	0.0	0.0	0.0	0.0	2.4

[a] r = 0.05, g = 0.015.
[b] Thousands ATS (1998 present values).
[c] Per capita shares in public deficit and government consumption included.

Chapter 3

Immigration and Income Redistribution - A Political Economy Analysis

3.1 Introduction

The importance of the subject of immigration, in particular in the course of increasing economic integration, is mirrored in an extensive literature. Within the last decade, an increasing amount of work has been dealing with the redistributive effects of immigration. The primary question there has been to what extent labour mobility might cause fiscal externalities arising with fiscal competition, and to what extent it might even hinder redistribution by national governments.[1] In these theoretical analyses, the political decision-making process is typically disregarded, and government policy is modelled with the help of interdepen-

[1] See for example Oates (1972) and Wildasin (1994).

dent utility functions of altruistic individuals or social planner considerations.

More recently however, several studies on the public economics of immigration have begun to refer to more realistic voting models of public policy. They take into account the impact that immigrants might have on redistributive outcomes by adding to the size of different interest groups and by thus changing the political constituency of the native population.[2] Along these lines, this chapter provides an analysis of the possible impact of immigrant participation on the voting outcome regarding the level of income redistribution. It is related to Razin and Sadka (2002) and Dolmas and Huffman (2003) in that it derives tax-voting equilibria under endogenous immigration within a median voter model. The migration and taxation equilibria are characterised as follows: immigration is induced by net income differentials between a foreign and a home country for a given tax rate, while the tax rate is (directly) voted upon by the new, enlarged population consisting of natives as well as immigrants. Both Razin and Sadka (2002) and Dolmas and Huffman (2003) find that the addition of immigrants who are both poorer than the native population and permitted to vote over redistribution does not necessarily result in higher taxes and transfers. In our model, multiple tax-transfer equilibria arise. That is, immigrants' votes can either increase or decrease the income tax rate. This depends on how homogeneous natives are in their skills. If they are relatively heterogeneous, natives would be against immigrant voting since it could alter voting outcomes and tilt the political balance to what would be to them an unfavourable (a non-optimal) level of redistribution. In a referendum, natives would therefore vote against giving immigrants the vote.

The model most importantly differs from Razin and Sadka (1997) by allowing for immigrants to be both skilled and unskilled, and

[2] See for example Mazza and van Winden (1996), Cremer and Pestieau (1998) and Razin and Sadka (1997).

by deriving tax-voting equilibria under immigration analytically. Dolmas and Huffman (2003) also only consider unskilled ('poor') immigrants, but incorporate effects on factor prices. Neither of these papers, however, explicitly addresses the following, closely related policy issue: the impact of immigrant voting on political outcomes as a possible determinant of the outcome of a native referendum on immigrant voting rights.

The model is a purely redistributive one and thus does not take into account possible welfare effects of immigration via different channels, for example public goods, social insurance[3] or the labour market[4]. Also, we had to restrict ourselves to the case of exogenous wages[5][6] in order to be able to derive equilibrium values analytically. Extensions in these directions pose a challenge for future research.

A further, rather straightforward result in this model is that unskilled natives will vote for (against) immigration if it increases (decreases) the overall percentage of skilled and thereby the net

[3]For example on pay-as-you-go financed pension systems via a favourable age distribution of immigrants (see for example OECD (1998a,b) and Razin and Sadka (1998, 1999a,b)).

[4]For example via the so-called 'immigration surplus' (see Borjas (1994, 1999)), assuming that wages are decreasing in immigration.

[5]In their model with endogenous education cost and resulting endogenous wages, Razin and Sadka (1997) resort to a numerical computation of voting equilibria.

[6]The assumption of exogenous wages does not seem so distressing the light of the fact that the effect of immigration on local labour market outcomes has been found to be, if at all, modest in empirical studies (see for example Altonji and Card (1991), Borjas, Freeman and Katz (1996), Card (1990, 2001), Kuhn and Wooton (1991), Lalonde and Topel (1991) for the US, Pischke and Velling (1994), de New and Zimmermann (1994, 1999) for Germany, Hunt (1992) for France, Winter-Ebmer and Zweimueller (1996, 1999) for Austria, Angrist and Kugler (2001) for Western Europe in general and, most recently, Dustmann et al. (2003) for the UK). Of course, this still abstracts from a possible labour supply adjustment taking place for example via the education decision (see for example Razin and Sadka (1997) and Casarico and Devillanova (2001)).

income of the unskilled[7], skilled natives will be indifferent towards immigration.[8] We derive the according result in a normative analysis of tax outcomes: the (utilitarian) social welfare of natives is maximised under a high (low) level of redistribution if mean income increases (decreases) with immigration.

The issue of immigration and immigrant voting is of high political interest and relevance. Welfare spending on immigrants ranges among the primary concerns of natives in regard to immigration in Europe[9], and the question of how (or rather, whether) to incorporate foreign citizens in political decision-making remains contentious. Although (legal) residents of foreign citizenship (henceforth called immigrants) are granted the economic rights and duties of working and contributing to and (to varying degrees) receiving welfare benefits, they are generally excluded from political decision-making at both local and national levels and therefore from decisions on how (much) taxes are to be paid and benefits are to be spent. Of the fifteen countries currently in the EU, only five countries (Denmark, Finland, Ireland, Netherlands, Sweden) automatically deliver voting rights to non-EU immigrants, usually at the local level, and non does at the national level, where the amount of fiscal redistribution is to a large part determined. This chapter undertakes to determine whether there is a case for natives to oppose or support immigrant voting out of redistributive concerns.

The chapter is organised as follows: Section 3.2 describes the model and Section 3.3 carries out the analysis of voting equilibria both for a closed (3.3.1) and an open economy (3.3.2) when

[7]This corresponds with the general empirical finding that the fiscal contribution of immigrants depends positively on their level of educational achievement (see for example OECD (1997)).

[8]A growing number of OECD countries have stressed the importance of the attraction of skilled immigrants in recent years (compare Coppel et al. (2001), p. 18).

[9]Compare the results of a quantitative analysis of parliamentary debates in European countries by Wodak (2000).

immigrants either can or cannot vote on the tax rate. Besides, the open economy analysis is extended for the case of two periods (3.3.3) and endogenous labour supply (3.3.4). In Section 3.4, we address the issue of a referendum among natives on immigration and on immigrant voting rights. Section 3.5 looks at the related literature and Section 3.6 concludes.

3.2 The model

3.2.1 The economy

There are two countries, home and foreign, with possible migration from the foreign to the home country. The time horizon considered is either one or two periods - a more detailed discussion follows in the next section. In each country, a single consumption good is produced only from labour input. In both countries, there are two types of workers: skilled and unskilled. Initially, we assume that each type of worker supplies one unit of labour at a reservation wage of zero. This assumption is relaxed when we consider endogenous labour supply in Section 3.3.4.

In the home country, high- and low-productivity workers differ in gross wages y_s and y_u, respectively (with $y_s > y_u$), which are exogenous. Similarly, in the foreign country, skilled and unskilled workers earn (given) net wages $\widetilde{y_s}$ and $\widetilde{y_u}$ (with $\widetilde{y_s} > \widetilde{y_u}$). Wages of a given type of worker are lower in the foreign country than in the home country. We consider an economy with perfect competition, wages are expressed in units of the consumption good and equal the marginal (and, in our case of perfectly inelastic labour supply, also the average) product of one unit of labour.

Because wages are lower in the foreign country, there is potential migration to the home country. The migration decision of immigrants is endogenous, depending on international present value net-income differentials and moving costs. Immigrants have heterogeneous moving costs c, and c is assumed to be uniformly distributed in the (foreign) population over $[0, \bar{c}]$. The timing of migration is discussed in Section 3.2.2 below.

The government is redistributing income by levying a flat rate income tax (t) and granting a lump-sum cash benefit (b). We assume that the government's budget must be balanced in each period. Natives and immigrants are treated alike fiscally: the tax revenue from the income tax t levied on unskilled and skilled labour income of both natives and immigrants is redistributed evenly through the lump-sum transfer b, which is granted to unskilled and skilled natives as well as immigrants. It is assumed that $0 \leq t \leq 1$: a negative tax rate that is effectively redistributing income from the poor to the rich is viewed to be socially unacceptable and implausible, whereas a tax rate $t > 1$ can be ruled out because people cannot be taxed by more than their total income. Until Section 3.3.4 we effectively assume individual labour supply to be fixed, the income tax does not therefore distort individual labour supply decisions.

3.2.2 Scenarios and timing of events

In the following analysis of the equilibrium tax rate, we consider three scenarios:

1. A closed economy, that is one in which there is no immigration possible. It is therefore only natives who vote upon the tax rate. This scenario serves as a base case scenario. In comparing outcomes between this one and the open-economy scenarios, we can determine whether immigration makes redistribution more or less likely.

2. An open economy in a one-period time frame with immigration at the beginning of the period. We analyse tax

equilibria for both the cases when immigrants are and when they are not allowed to vote on the tax rate.

3. An open economy in a two-period time frame with again possible immigration at the beginning of the first period. Immigrants are not allowed to participate in voting on the tax rate of the first period, but are only allowed to vote on the tax rate of the second period. We are interested in the effect that delayed voting rights have on the tax outcome. The idea is that immigration incentives and therefore equilibrium results might change if immigrants cannot participate in voting from the beginning of their arrival.[10] We will see that the basic results of scenario 2) stay unchanged.

Below, we will now determine our two endogenous variables, the immigration rate and the tax rate. Assumptions are such that the tax rate is determined in a direct democracy process by the median voter (that is, the voter with median pre-tax income). It will be the one maximising the median voter's net income. Median voter income, however, will change with immigration, which is taking place according to international present value net-income differentials and moving costs, as mentioned above.

3.3 Analysis

3.3.1 Closed economy

The proportion of skilled and unskilled natives is λ_s^n, λ_u^n, respectively, with

$$\lambda_s^n + \lambda_u^n = 1. \tag{3.1}$$

[10] Compare the demand for delayed participation of immigrants in welfare schemes, which is sometimes raised (see for example Sinn (2002)).

The government budget constraint requires that total expenditure via lump-sum grants is equal to total tax revenue - or, equivalently, that per capita grant equals average tax payment:

$$b = t\left(\lambda_s^n y_s + \lambda_u^n y_u\right). \tag{3.2}$$

Individuals seek to maximise their utility given by their net income:

$$v_i(t) = (1-t)y_i + b \quad i = s, u,$$

or, after substituting in for b:

$$v_s(t) = y_s - t\lambda_u^n(y_s - y_u), \tag{3.3}$$

$$v_u(t) = y_u + t\lambda_s^n(y_s - y_u). \tag{3.4}$$

One can now see that the skilled prefer a tax rate of 0 (assuming that $t \geq 0$), whereas the unskilled prefer a tax rate of 1. Depending on whether there is a majority of skilled or unskilled in the population, the outcome of majority voting on the tax rate will be 0 or 1:

$$t^* = \begin{cases} 0 & if \quad \lambda_u^n \leq 0.5 \\ 1 & if \quad \lambda_u^n > 0.5. \end{cases} \tag{3.5}$$

It is worth noting that the tax rate of 1 is an extreme consequence of the assumption of exogenous labour supply together with zero cost of taxation. Only then, an unskilled majority would vote for the total taxation of income and redistribution that results in an equalisation of net income across the whole population.[11]

[11] As soon as we relax the assumption of exogenous labour supply, we will find an upper limitation of the tax rate $\bar{t} < 1$. For more on this case see Section 3.3.4.

3.3.2 One-period open economy

Migration

In the open economy, we now allow for immigration to take place - so let us first have a look at how migration decisions are determined.

Immigration is induced by the income gap between the net present value of income in the foreign country (net of moving cost) and the net present value of income in the home country. So, there exists a cut-off level of moving cost c for skilled and unskilled migrants, $\widetilde{c_s}$ and $\widetilde{c_u}$, respectively, such that all those with moving cost below $\widetilde{c_s}$ or $\widetilde{c_u}$ migrate, and all the others remain in their country of origin.

Given the cut-offs, the amount of skilled immigration λ_s^m and unskilled immigration λ_u^m is therefore determined by migration costs in the following way (remember that the moving costs $\widetilde{c_s}$ and $\widetilde{c_u}$ are uniformly distributed over $[0, \overline{c_s}]$ and $[0, \overline{c_u}]$, respectively:

$$\lambda_s^m = \frac{\widetilde{c_s}}{\overline{c}}, \tag{3.6}$$

$$\lambda_u^m = \frac{\widetilde{c_u}}{\overline{c}}. \tag{3.7}$$

To simplify notation, we will set $\overline{c_s} = \overline{c_u} \equiv 1$ from now on.[12]

The cut-offs $\widetilde{c_s}$ and $\widetilde{c_u}$ are defined to equal net income differentials. This is because given free mobility, migrants are indifferent between moving or not when the net income gain from moving is equal to their moving cost.

[12]Note that in doing so, we implicitly assume that the skilled and the unskilled subpopulations in the foreign country are of the same size and equal to 1, respectively. For a derivation of results in the case of different foreign subpopulation sizes, which remain unchanged, see Appendix 3.A.

$$\widetilde{c_s} \equiv (1 - t^*)\, y_s + b^* - \widetilde{y_s}, \tag{3.8}$$

$$\widetilde{c_u} \equiv (1 - t^*)\, y_u + b^* - \widetilde{y_u}. \tag{3.9}$$

Hence,

$$\lambda_s^m \equiv (1 - t^*)\, y_s + b^* - \widetilde{y_s}, \tag{3.10}$$

$$\lambda_u^m \equiv (1 - t^*)\, y_u + b^* - \widetilde{y_u}. \tag{3.11}$$

Note that the cut-offs, and therefore immigration, depend on taxes and benefits in the foreign country. When immigrants find the net income difference to outweigh their migration cost, they migrate, otherwise they do not.

It can be seen that in this case, where migration costs are introduced, migrants do care about the tax rate even when there is free migration. In contrast, in a case of free migration and no migration costs, net income differentials would be zero and immigrant income would always be the equal to given foreign net income $\widetilde{y_s}$ and $\widetilde{y_u}$, regardless of the tax rate t and the implied transfer b prevailing in the home country. Immigrants would therefore not care about participating in the political process of the home country.[13]

Preferences over taxes

With immigration, the skill composition of the population is likely to change. The proportion of skilled and unskilled in the home country after immigration is now $\lambda_s^n + \lambda_s^m$ and $\lambda_u^n + \lambda_u^m$, respectively, with a total population of $1 + \lambda_s^m + \lambda_u^m$.

[13]See Razin and Sadka (1997).

As in the closed economy scenario above, we require the government budget to be balanced and therefore per capita grant to equal average tax payment:

$$b^* = t^*[(\lambda_s^n + \lambda_s^m)y_s + (\lambda_u^n + \lambda_u^m)y_u]/(1 + \lambda_s^m + \lambda_u^m). \quad (3.12)$$

Individuals' utility is again given by their net income:

$$v_i(t) = (1-t)y_i + b \quad i = s, u.$$

After inserting the budget constraint and restructuring, we get

$$v_s(t) = y_s - t(y_s - y_u)(\lambda_u^n + \lambda_u^m)/(1 + \lambda_s^m + \lambda_u^m), \quad (3.13)$$

$$v_u(t) = y_u + t(y_s - y_u)(\lambda_s^n + \lambda_s^m)/(1 + \lambda_s^m + \lambda_u^m). \quad (3.14)$$

Individuals prefer the tax rate that maximises their utility, so as in the closed-economy case, the skilled prefer a tax rate of 0 (assuming that $t \geq 0$), whereas the unskilled prefer a tax rate of 1. Depending on whether there is a majority of skilled or unskilled in the population, the outcome of majority voting on the tax rate will thus be either 0 or 1.

Equilibrium

A *political equilibrium* is a vector $(t^*, b^*, \lambda_u^m, \lambda_s^m)$ such that (i) t^* is the choice of the median voter, given λ_u^m, λ_s^m (ii) b^* is satisfying the government budget constraint, given $t^*, \lambda_u^m, \lambda_s^m$ and (iii) λ_u^m, λ_s^m are determined as described in the section on migration above, given t^*, b^*. The identity of the median voter will depend upon whether migrants can vote or not.

Migrants cannot vote

If migrants cannot vote, the skilled will be in majority if

$$\lambda_u^n < 0.5,$$

the unskilled will be in majority if

$$\lambda_u^n > 0.5,$$

and the conditions for the outcome of the tax vote to be 0 or 1 are:

$$t^* = \begin{cases} 0 & if \quad \lambda_u^n \leq 0.5 \\ 1 & if \quad \lambda_u^n > 0.5 \end{cases} \tag{3.15}$$

This is the same outcome as in the closed economy. Again, this is a consequence of our assumption of exogenous labour supply, since with the introduction of tax distortion where we have a diminishing labour supply and tax base, the optimal tax rate will not only be upper-limited at some $\overline{t} < 1$, but will also depend upon the relation between mean and median income, which might change with immigration even if immigrants are not allowed to vote because mean income in the population can change. In this case, therefore, immigrants, through their impact on the labour market, might still change the optimal level of redistribution and the outcome of the tax vote.[14]

Migrants can vote

If migrants can vote, the skilled will be in majority if

$$\lambda_u^n + \lambda_u^m < 0.5(1 + \lambda_s^m + \lambda_u^m),$$

and the unskilled will be in majority if

$$\lambda_u^n + \lambda_u^m > 0.5(1 + \lambda_s^m + \lambda_u^m).$$

The conditions for the outcome of the tax vote to be 0 or 1 therefore are :

[14]See Section 3.3.4.

$$t^* = \begin{cases} 0 & if \quad \lambda_u^n + \lambda_u^m \leq 0.5(1 + \lambda_s^m + \lambda_u^m) \\ 1 & if \quad \lambda_u^n + \lambda_u^m > 0.5(1 + \lambda_s^m + \lambda_u^m) \end{cases} \tag{3.16}$$

Proposition 1. *If migrants can vote, there is a political equilibrium with no redistribution* ($t = 0$) *if* $\lambda_u^n \leq 0.5[1 + (y_s - y_u) - (\widetilde{y_s} - \widetilde{y_u})] \equiv \lambda_u^n(0)$ *and one with redistribution* ($t = 1$) *if* $\lambda_u^n > 0.5$ $[1 - (\widetilde{y_s} - \widetilde{y_u})] \equiv \lambda_u^n(1)$. *Therefore, we always have multiple political equilibria when* $\lambda_u^n(1) < \lambda_u^n \leq \lambda_u^n(0)$.

Proof. Recall that for $t^* = 0$, it has to be true that

$$\lambda_u^n + \lambda_u^m \leq 0.5(1 + \lambda_s^m + \lambda_u^m),$$

or, after restructuring:

$$\lambda_u^n \leq 0.5(1 + \lambda_s^m - \lambda_u^m). \tag{3.17}$$

Using (3.10) and (3.11) as well as the fact that $t = 0$ (and $b = 0$, using (3.12)), the equilibrium conditions determining the migration rate of skilled and unskilled immigrants, respectively, are the following:

$$y_s - \widetilde{y_s} = \lambda_s^m, \tag{3.18}$$

$$y_u - \widetilde{y_u} = \lambda_u^m. \tag{3.19}$$

The condition for the tax rate to be zero therefore is

$$\lambda_u^n \leq 0.5\,[1 + (y_s - y_u) - (\widetilde{y_s} - \widetilde{y_u})] \equiv \lambda_u^n(0). \tag{3.20}$$

For $t^* = 1$, it has to be true that

$$\lambda_u^n + \lambda_u^m > 0.5(1 + \lambda_s^m + \lambda_u^m),$$

or, after restructuring:

$$\lambda_u^n > 0.5(1 + \lambda_s^m - \lambda_u^m). \tag{3.21}$$

As above, immigration is determined by net income differentials between the foreign and the home country.

If $t^* = 1$, tax revenue is equal to total income in the population (taxation is assumed to be costless) and is then distributed equally through lump-sum transfers, so that wages in the destination country will be equalised, and arbitrage conditions are the following:

$$[(\lambda_s^n + \lambda_s^m)y_s + (\lambda_u^n + \lambda_u^m)y_u]/(1 + \lambda_s^m + \lambda_u^m) - \widetilde{y_s} = \lambda_s^m, \tag{3.22}$$

$$[(\lambda_s^n + \lambda_s^m)y_s + (\lambda_u^n + \lambda_u^m)y_u]/(1 + \lambda_s^m + \lambda_u^m) - \widetilde{y_u} = \lambda_u^m. \tag{3.23}$$

Therefore,

$$\lambda_u^m - \lambda_s^m = \widetilde{y_s} - \widetilde{y_u}, \tag{3.24}$$

and we get the following condition for the tax rate to be one:

$$\lambda_u^n > 0.5\,[1 - (\widetilde{y_s} - \widetilde{y_u})] \equiv \lambda_u^n(1). \tag{3.25}$$

QED.

These multiple equilibria arise because immigration will always be such that the tax rate that immigrants are taking as given when deciding to migrate will be the one preferred by the (new) majority. There are two possibilities: either immigrants believe in a tax rate of 0 - then, immigration will indeed be such that a majority of immigrants and natives will vote for a tax rate of 0. Or, immigrants believe in a tax rate of 1 - then, immigration will be such that a majority will vote for a tax rate of 1. Since immigrants make up part of the new majority, both a tax rate of zero and one is compatible with immigration - if the skill composition of natives is not too homogeneous and their majority therefore is not too strong.

In comparing the open-economy values of required majorities $\lambda_u^n(0)$ and $\lambda_u^n(1)$ with their closed-economy equivalents, we can answer the question of whether allowing migration makes a redistribution outcome more likely or less likely.

If $(y_s - y_u) < (\widetilde{y_s} - \widetilde{y_u})$, we have $\lambda_u^n(0) < 0.5$. The gross income advantage is smaller for the skilled, and it is predominantly unskilled immigrants who join the native population and vote for a tax rate of 1 together with unskilled natives. The minimum proportion of unskilled natives necessary for a pro tax vote is now smaller than in the closed economy, and redistribution becomes more likely.

3.3.3 Two-period open economy

In our third scenario, we evaluate voting equilibria with immigration and two periods, when immigrants are allowed to vote in the second, but not in the first period. They take the first-period tax rate (which is voted upon by natives only) as given and take into account the present value of net income in both periods when deciding on migration. Thus, we seek to determine whether it makes a difference for natives if immigrants are allowed to vote at once or only after a first period.

For this case of two periods, we have to review the relevant cut-offs determining immigration. As before, they are determined by aggregate present value net income differentials, whereby the first-period tax-transfer scheme t_1^*, b_1^* is taken as given:

$$\widetilde{c_s} \equiv \left\{ \left[(1 - t_1^*)\, y_s + b_1^* \right] + \left[\frac{(1 - t_2^*) y_s + b_2^*}{(1+r)} \right] \right\} - \left[\widetilde{y_s} + \frac{\widetilde{y_s}}{(1+r)} \right] \tag{3.26}$$

$$\widetilde{c_u} \equiv \left\{ \left[(1 - t_1^*)\, y_u + b_1^* \right] + \left[\frac{(1 - t_2^*) y_u + b_2^*}{(1+r)} \right] \right\} - \left[\widetilde{y_u} + \frac{\widetilde{y_u}}{(1+r)} \right] \tag{3.27}$$

In the following, we assume $r = 0$.

Tax preferences and majority requirements will be as before, and we can determine the *political equilibrium* analogously to derive the following

Proposition 2. *If migrants can vote after one period, there is a political equilibrium with no redistribution* ($t_2^* = 0$) *if* $\lambda_u^n \leq 0.5\,[1 - 2(\widetilde{y_s} - \widetilde{y_u}) + (2 - t_1^*)(y_s - y_u)] \equiv \lambda_u^n(0)$ *and one with redistribution* ($t_2^* = 1$) *if* $\lambda_u^n > 0.5\,[1 - 2(\widetilde{y_s} - \widetilde{y_u}) + (1 - t_1^*)(y_s - y_u)] \equiv \lambda_u^n(1)$. *Therefore, we always have multiple political equilibria when* $\lambda_u^n(1) < \lambda_u^n \leq \lambda_u^n(0)$.

Proof. Recall that, for $t_2^* = 0$, it has to be true that

$$\lambda_u^n \leq 0.5(1 + \lambda_s^m - \lambda_u^m).$$

Using (3.26) and (3.27) as well as the fact that $t_2^* = 0$, we get the following equilibrium conditions for immigration:

$$[(1 - t_1^*) y_s + b_1^*] + y_s - 2\widetilde{y_s} = \lambda_s^m, \tag{3.28}$$

$$[(1 - t_1^*) y_u + b_1^*] + y_u - 2\widetilde{y_u} = \lambda_u^m. \tag{3.29}$$

It therefore has to be true that

$$\lambda_u^n \leq 0.5\,[1 - 2(\widetilde{y_s} - \widetilde{y_u}) + (2 - t_1^*)(y_s - y_u)] \equiv \lambda_u^n(0). \quad (3.30)$$

For $t_2^* = 1$, it has to be true that

$$\lambda_u^n > 0.5(1 + \lambda_s^m - \lambda_u^m).$$

Cut-offs and therefore immigration are determined as follows:

$$[(1-t_1^*)y_s+b_1^*]+[(\lambda_s^n+\lambda_s^m)y_s+(\lambda_u^n+\lambda_u^m)y_u]/(1+\lambda_s^m+\lambda_u^m)- \quad (3.31)$$
$$-2\widetilde{y_s} = \lambda_s^m,$$

$$[(1-t_1^*)y_u+b_1^*]+[(\lambda_s^n+\lambda_s^m)y_s+(\lambda_u^n+\lambda_u^m)y_u]/(1+\lambda_s^m+\lambda_u^m)- \quad (3.32)$$
$$-2\widetilde{y_u} = \lambda_u^m.$$

It therefore has to be true that

$$\lambda_u^n > 0.5\,[1 - 2(\widetilde{y_s} - \widetilde{y_u}) + (1 - t_1)(y_s - y_u)] \equiv \lambda_u^n(1). \quad (3.33)$$

The rationing for the multiple equilibria outcome is the same as above.

Again, we can determine conditions under which a redistribution outcome becomes more or less likely:

Redistribution becomes less likely if $(1-t_1)(y_s-y_u) > 2(\widetilde{y_s}-\widetilde{y_u})$, since then we have $\lambda_u^n(1) > 0.5$, and the minimum proportion of unskilled natives necessary for a pro tax vote increases.

Redistribution becomes less likely if $(2-t_1)(y_s-y_u) < 2(\widetilde{y_s}-\widetilde{y_u})$, since then we have $\lambda_u^n(0) < 0.5$, and the minimum proportion of unskilled natives for a pro tax vote decreases.

Next, we want to relax the assumption of exogenous labour supply and see whether our basic conclusions still hold.

3.3.4 Endogenous labour supply and the open economy

With labour supply being endogenous, that is, dependent on the tax rate, the optimal tax rate will be lower than 1 because too high a tax exerts a negative incentive effect on the provision of labour. To determine the optimal income tax t for individuals with endogenous labour supply $L(t)$, we again maximise individuals' indirect utility $v(t,b)$:[15]

$$v_i(t,b) = 0.5 + b + 0.5(1-t)^2 w_i^2,$$

with respect to the same budget constraint $b(t)$:

$$b^*(\lambda_u^m, \lambda_s^m) = t^*[(\lambda_s^n + \lambda_s^m)y_s + (\lambda_u^n + \lambda_u^m)y_u]/(1+\lambda_s^m+\lambda_u^m). \quad (3.34)$$

This yields the following expression for the optimal income tax $t(\lambda_s^m, \lambda_u^m)$[16]:

$$t_i^* = \frac{\frac{1}{(1+\lambda_s^m+\lambda_u^m)}[(\lambda_s^n + \lambda_s^m)y_s + (\lambda_u^n + \lambda_u^m)y_u] - y_i}{2\frac{1}{(1+\lambda_s^m+\lambda_u^m)}[(\lambda_s^n + \lambda_s^m)y_s + (\lambda_u^n + \lambda_u^m)y_u] + y_i}, \qquad i = s, u. \quad (3.35)$$

We can see that individuals' optimal level of the tax rate depends on the difference between their income and mean income. The lower their own income relative to mean income, the higher the tax rate they prefer. Adversely, with increasing income individuals' preferred tax rate decreases to zero when their income is equal to mean income. Imposing the restriction that $t \geq 0$, individuals' preferred tax rate will be zero if their income is equal to or higher than mean income.

[15]See Appendix 3.B for derivation.

[16]See the derivation of (3.65) in Appendix 3.B.

Equilibrium

As before, with majority voting the tax rate will be determined by the median voter, who chooses the one which maximises his or her utility. Depending on whether the median voter is skilled or unskilled, the outcome of majority voting on the tax rate will be 0 or positive but smaller than 1.

If migrants cannot vote,
the median voter will be skilled if

$$\lambda_u^n < 0.5,$$

and the median voter will be unskilled if

$$\lambda_u^n > 0.5.$$

Hence, again assuming that $y_s > y_u$ and $t \geq 0$, the tax outcome will be:

$$t^*(\lambda_u^m, \lambda_s^m) = \left\{ \begin{array}{c} 0 \\ \frac{\frac{1}{(1+\lambda_s^m+\lambda_u^m)}[(\lambda_u^n+\lambda_u^m)y_u+(1-\lambda_u^n+\lambda_s^m)y_s]-y_u}{2\frac{1}{(1+\lambda_s^m+\lambda_u^m)}[(\lambda_u^n+\lambda_u^m)y_u+(1-\lambda_u^n+\lambda_s^m)y_s]+y_u} \end{array} \right. \tag{3.36}$$

$$if \quad \left\{ \begin{array}{c} \lambda_u^n \leq 0.5 \\ \lambda_u^n > 0.5. \end{array} \right.$$

If migrants can vote,
the median voter will be skilled if

$$\lambda_u^n + \lambda_u^m < 0.5(1 + \lambda_s^m + \lambda_u^m),$$

and the median voter will be unskilled if

$$\lambda_u^n + \lambda_u^m < 0.5(1 + \lambda_s^m + \lambda_u^m).$$

The tax outcome then will be:

$$t^*(\lambda_u^m, \lambda_s^m) = \left\{ \begin{array}{c} 0 \\ \frac{\frac{1}{(1+\lambda_s^m+\lambda_u^m)}[(\lambda_u^n+\lambda_u^m)y_u+(1-\lambda_u^n+\lambda_s^m)y_s]-y_u}{2\frac{1}{(1+\lambda_s^m+\lambda_u^m)}[(\lambda_u^n+\lambda_u^m)y_u+(1-\lambda_u^n+\lambda_s^m)y_s]+y_u} \end{array} \right. \tag{3.37}$$

$$if \quad \left\{ \begin{array}{c} \lambda_u^n + \lambda_u^m \leq 0.5(1 + \lambda_s^m + \lambda_u^m) \\ \lambda_u^n + \lambda_u^m > 0.5(1 + \lambda_s^m + \lambda_u^m). \end{array} \right.$$

We see that now, unlike in the case of exogenous labour supply, immigration might not only change the equilibrium lump-sum grant, but also the tax voting outcome even if immigrants are not allowed to vote: the preferred tax rate of the unskilled is increasing in mean income and decreasing in median income: if mean income increases by more than median income, the preferred tax rate increases, if mean income decreases by more than median income, the preferred tax rate decreases.[17]

Proposition 3. *With endogenous labour supply, if migrants can vote, there is a political equilibrium with no redistribution* ($t = 0$) *if* $\lambda_u^n \leq 0.5\left[1 + (y_s - y_u) - (\widetilde{y_s} - \widetilde{y_u})\right] \equiv \lambda_u^n(0)$ *and one with positive redistribution* ($0 < t < 1$) *if* $\lambda_u^n > 0.5[1+(1-t)(y_s-y_u)-(\widetilde{y_s} - \widetilde{y_u})] \equiv \lambda_u^n(+)$. *Therefore, we always have multiple political equilibria when* $\lambda_u^n(+) < \lambda_u^n \leq \lambda_u^n(0)$.

Proof. As before in (3.20), for $t^* = 0$, the skilled have to be in majority:

$$\lambda_u^n \leq 0.5(1 + \lambda_s^m - \lambda_u^m).$$

To determine the equilibrium levels of immigration, we need to proceed in the same way as above, using (3.37) and (3.34) and

[17] In a model with exogenous labour supply but endogenous skill acquisition, Razin and Sadka (1997) find the mean income effect dominating: the optimal level of the tax rate is found to be decreasing with unskilled immigration.

solving (3.10) and (3.11) for t^*, b^*, λ_s^m and λ_u^m. The only difference to be kept in mind is that now, the optimal tax rate depends on not only on median, but also on mean income and therefore on immigration, we write $t^*(\lambda_u^m, \lambda_s^m)$:

$$(1 - t^*(\lambda_u^m, \lambda_s^m))y_s + b^*(\lambda_u^m, \lambda_s^m) - \widetilde{y_s} = \lambda_s^m, \tag{3.38}$$

$$(1 - t^*(\lambda_u^m, \lambda_s^m))y_u + b^*(\lambda_u^m, \lambda_s^m) - \widetilde{y_u} = \lambda_u^m. \tag{3.39}$$

For $t = 0$, nothing changes, and equilibrium migration levels are again:

$$y_s - \widetilde{y_s} = \lambda_s^m,$$

and

$$y_u - \widetilde{y_u} = \lambda_u^m.$$

As before, the condition for the tax rate to be zero therefore is:

$$\lambda_u^n \leq 0.5\left[1 + (y_s - y_u) - (\widetilde{y_s} - \widetilde{y_u})\right] \equiv \lambda_u^n(0). \tag{3.40}$$

For $0 < t^* < 1$, the unskilled have to be in majority:

$$\lambda_u^n > 0.5(1 + \lambda_s^m - \lambda_u^m).$$

Now, from looking at (3.38) and (3.39) we can see that we cannot solve for equilibrium levels analytically in this case, since t^* and therefore b^* depend on λ_s^m and λ_u^m and vice versa. However, we can still determine whether we have multiple political equilibria or not:

From (3.38) and (3.39), we get the following:

$$\lambda_s^m - \lambda_u^m = (1 - t^*(\lambda_u^m, \lambda_s^m))(y_s - y_u) - (\widetilde{y_s} - \widetilde{y_u}). \tag{3.41}$$

The condition for the tax rate to be positive (but smaller than one) therefore is:

$$\lambda_u^n > 0.5\left[1 + (1 - t^*(\lambda_u^m, \lambda_s^m))(y_s - y_u) - (\widetilde{y_s} - \widetilde{y_u})\right] \equiv \lambda_u^n(+). \tag{3.42}$$

Since we know that $0 < t^*(\lambda_u^m, \lambda_s^m) < 1$, we have $\lambda_u^n(+) < \lambda_u^n(0)$.

Q.E.D.

3.4 Is immigration and immigrant voting desirable for natives?

In the analyses above, we derived two main results: firstly, with immigrant voting, multiple voting equilibria arise with respect to the tax-transfer policy, and secondly, immigrant voting can change native majority requirements to a level above or below the ones in a closed economy and thus make redistribution more or less likely.

Now, we can determine whether the majority of natives gains or loses from immigration and immigrant voting and whether therefore, in a referendum, they would vote for or against it:

Proposition 4. *In a native referendum by majority rule on whether to give immigrants the vote, natives vote 'no' if 1)* $\lambda_u^n(1) < \lambda_u^n < \lambda_u^n(0)$ *or 2)* $0.5 < \lambda_u^n < \lambda_u^n(1)$ *or 3)* $\lambda_u^n(0) < \lambda_u^n < 0.5$. *The outcome of the referendum is indeterminate in all other cases.*

Proof. The tax rate can change with immigrant voting given any of the three conditions above. In 1), the tax outcome is indeterminate due to multiple equilibria. In 2), the majority required for a tax rate of one increases, so the voting outcome will change if the unskilled majority is not strong enough. In 3), the analogue is true for a skilled majority. If immigrant voting changes the tax rate, then by definition, the majority of natives will be worse off. Given immigration, the majority of natives will be worse off, if immigrant voting changes the tax rate.[18] Assuming that natives are not only against a definite but also against a - due to multiple voting equilibria - possible change in the tax rate, natives would therefore vote against immigrant voting rights in each of the two cases above. If the tax rate is not changed, natives will be indifferent, and the referendum outcome would be indeterminate.

Proposition 5. *In a native referendum by majority rule on whether to allow immigration, the outcome is indeterminate for* $\lambda_u^n < 0.5$. *For* $\lambda_u^n > 0.5$, *natives vote 'yes' if* $\frac{\lambda_s^m}{\lambda_u^m} > \frac{\lambda_s^n}{\lambda_u^n}$ *and 'no' if* $\frac{\lambda_s^m}{\lambda_u^m} < \frac{\lambda_s^n}{\lambda_u^n}$. *The outcome is indeterminate if* $\frac{\lambda_s^m}{\lambda_u^m} = \frac{\lambda_s^n}{\lambda_u^n}$.

Proof. Natives' utility is affected by immigration, even if immigrants are not allowed to vote on the tax rate, via a change in mean income, which affects the lump-sum transfer b^*.

According to the skill composition of the native population, we can distinguish the following two cases:

1. For $\lambda_u^n < 0.5$, there is no redistribution ($t^* = 0$ and $b^* = 0$), and the native (skilled) majority is indifferent.

2. For $\lambda_u^n > 0.5$, there is redistribution ($t^* = 1$), and the native (unskilled) majority will be against (in favour) of immigration, if b^* goes down (up). From looking at the government budget constraints of the open and the closed economy, (3.12) and (3.2), we can see that this is the case if with immigration, the aggregate proportion of skilled decreases (increases), that is iff $\frac{\lambda_s^n+\lambda_s^m}{1+\lambda_s^m+\lambda_u^m} < \lambda_s^n$ ($\frac{\lambda_s^n+\lambda_s^m}{1+\lambda_s^m+\lambda_u^m} > \lambda_s^n$)

[18]This is because the prevailing tax rate is utility-maximising for the median voter and therefore the majority of natives.

or, equivalently, iff $\frac{\lambda_s^m}{\lambda_u^m} < \frac{\lambda_s^n}{\lambda_u^n}$ ($\frac{\lambda_s^m}{\lambda_u^m} > \frac{\lambda_s^n}{\lambda_u^n}$). The lump-sum transfer b^* will stay constant if immigration is such that $\frac{\lambda_s^m}{\lambda_u^m} = \frac{\lambda_s^n}{\lambda_u^n}$. In this case, the native majority will be indifferent.

Proposition 4'. *With endogenous labour supply, in a native referendum by majority rule on whether to give immigrants the vote, natives vote 'no' if 1) $\lambda_u^n(+) < \lambda_u^n < \lambda_u^n(0)$ or 2) $0.5 < \lambda_u^n < \lambda_u^n(+)$ or 3) $\lambda_u^n(0) < \lambda_u^n < 0.5$. They are indifferent in all other cases.*

Proof. As in Proposition 4 above, given immigration, the majority of natives will be worse off, if immigrant voting changes the tax rate. Although now, the optimal tax rate can change with immigration[19], a skilled (unskilled) majority will still always prefer a zero (positive) tax rate[20]and will oppose any according change in the voting outcome.

Proposition 5'. *With endogenous labour supply, in a native referendum by majority rule on whether to allow immigration, the outcome is indeterminate for $\lambda_u^n < 0.5$. For $\lambda_u^n > 0.5$, natives vote 'yes' if $\frac{\lambda_s^m}{\lambda_u^m} > \frac{\lambda_s^n}{\lambda_u^n}$ and 'no' if $\frac{\lambda_s^m}{\lambda_u^m} < \frac{\lambda_s^n}{\lambda_u^n}$. The outcome is indeterminate if $\frac{\lambda_s^m}{\lambda_u^m} = \frac{\lambda_s^n}{\lambda_u^n}$.*

Proof. Natives' utility is affected by immigration even in the absence of immigrant voting rights via a change in mean income, which affects the tax level optimal for natives t^* as well as the lump-sum transfer b^*.[21]

[19] Compare the formula for the optimal tax rate in (3.35).

[20] This is because mean income will always be below (above) median income of $y_s(y_u)$ with a skilled (unskilled) native majority.

[21] Note that, since wages are exogenous and immigrants are not allowed to vote, immigration has no impact on median voter income, and changes in the optimal level of the tax rate are solely due to changes in mean income.

According to the skill composition of the native population, we can distinguish between the following two cases:

1) For $\lambda_u^n < 0.5$, there is no redistribution ($t^* = 0$ and $b^* = 0$), and the native (skilled) majority is indifferent. It does not care about the skill mix of immigrants.[22]

2) For $\lambda_u^n > 0.5$, immigration does not change mean income and the tax rate if $\frac{\lambda_s^m}{\lambda_u^m} = \frac{\lambda_s^n}{\lambda_u^n}$. In this case, the native (unskilled) majority is indifferent because immigration does not change the skill mix. Immigration changes the preferred level of a positive tax rate of natives if mean income changes. The unskilled native majority will vote for immigration if $\frac{\lambda_s^m}{\lambda_u^m} > \frac{\lambda_s^n}{\lambda_u^n}$ and mean income, and thus t^* and b^*, increase. Similarly, it will be against immigration if $\frac{\lambda_s^m}{\lambda_u^m} < \frac{\lambda_s^n}{\lambda_u^n}$ and mean income, and thus t^* and b^*, decrease.[23]

To sum up, both in the case of exogenous and endogenous labour supply, an unskilled native majority will be for (against) immigration, if mean income increases (decreases), that is if immigrants are relatively more (less) skilled than natives. A skilled majority will be indifferent towards immigration. If, however, immigrants' voting power might alter the outcome of the tax vote t, natives will always be against immigrant voting.

3.5 Related literature

Other studies have also used a political economy approach to analyse the effect of immigration on public policy variables of the host country to prove that, in contrast to predictions of tax

[22]Note that as immigration has no impact on median voter income, it cannot change the preferred level of the tax rate from zero to positive. For this to happen, mean income would have to rise from below to above median income which is constant at y_s. (see Proof of Proposition 4' above)

[23]For the same reason as above, immigrants cannot change the preferred level of the tax rate from positive to zero. For this to happen, mean income would have to fall from above to below median income which is constant at y_u. (see Proof of Proposition 4' above)

competition theory, immigration does not have to lead to an erosion of the welfare state. For example, Mazza and van Winden (1996) find that transfers and disposable income for mobile workers can increase with immigration. Kemnitz (2002) shows that low skilled immigration can lead to higher unemployment benefits. Razin et al. (1998) find that unskilled migration may lead to a lower tax and less redistribution. Their paper, as well as the one by Dolmas and Huffman (2003), is perhaps most closely related to this chapter, since it also analyses thc interaction between migration and the political-economy equilibrium tax-transfer policy in the host country. There, too, net income differentials induce immigration, which changes the median voter's income and tax preference.

The present chapter is different in that it allows for both skilled and unskilled immigrants and analytically derives the conditions for a high-tax and a low-tax equilibrium. It is shown that immigration is compatible with both a high and a low tax rate, depending on the skill composition of natives.

3.6 Conclusion

The aim of this chapter was to determine the effect of immigration on the level of income redistribution via majority voting, given that immigration is endogenous and immigrants can be both skilled and unskilled. The tax outcome depends on the skill composition of natives and the initial amount of redistribution in the economy, which in turn determines the skill composition of immigrants. Accordingly, if immigrants are allowed to vote, they might either join the high-redistribution interest group (the unskilled) or the low-redistribution interest group (the skilled). It is found, firstly, that the probability for redistribution can increase or decrease and secondly, that for certain skill compositions of natives, both a high and a low equilibrium tax rate is compatible with immigration. Immigrant voting can then change the political majority. As a consequence, we can determine the gainers and losers within the native community from an extension of the franchise. If immigrant voting can change the political majority, the majority of natives can end up with a tax rate that makes them worse off. They will then oppose an extension of the franchise to immigrants, and a corresponding referendum would be defeated. For a percentage of skilled or unskilled natives above a certain threshold, however, immigrant voting does not matter for the outcome of the vote.

Non-citizen voting on a national level is currently denied in all European Union countries. According to the findings in this chapter, natives will oppose immigrant voting if their majority on the level of income redistribution is not strong enough. At best, natives are indifferent towards immigrant voting. As far as immigration itself is concerned, a native majority would gain from it and therefore vote for it, if it itself was unskilled and immigrants were relatively higher skilled than natives.

3.A Foreign population size.

3.A.1 One-period open economy: exogenous labour supply.

If we want to allow for a size of the skilled and unskilled foreign subpopulations unequal to 1, our characterization of multiple voting equilibria changes in the following way:

We now have skilled and unskilled immigration of the size

$$\lambda_s^m = \theta \frac{\widetilde{c_s}}{\overline{c_s}}, \tag{3.43}$$

and

$$\lambda_u^m = \varphi \frac{\widetilde{c_u}}{\overline{c_u}}, \tag{3.44}$$

where θ and φ are the factors determining the total number of foreign skilled and unskilled, and $\theta, \varphi \in R_+$.

Assuming that $\overline{c_s} = \overline{c_u} = 1$, and substituting for $\widetilde{c_s}$ and $\widetilde{c_u}$[24], we get

$$\lambda_s^m \equiv \theta \left[(1-t^*)y_s + b^* - \widetilde{y_s}\right], \tag{3.45}$$

and

$$\lambda_u^m \equiv \varphi \left[(1-t^*)y_u + b^* - \widetilde{y_u}\right]. \tag{3.46}$$

If migrants can vote, the equilibrium tax rate will be zero, if

$$\lambda_u^n \leq 0.5(1 + \lambda_s^m - \lambda_u^m),$$

or, substituting for λ_s^m and λ_u^m,

$$\lambda_u^n \leq 0.5\left[1 + \theta(y_s - \widetilde{y_s}) - \varphi(y_u - \widetilde{y_u})\right] \equiv \lambda_u^n(0). \tag{3.47}$$

[24]See (3.8) and (3.9).

For the equilibrium tax rate to be one, it must be true that

$$\lambda_u^n > 0.5(1 + \lambda_s^m - \lambda_u^m),$$

and that therefore

$$\lambda_u^n > 0.5\left[1 + \theta(\overline{y} - \widetilde{y_s}) - \varphi(\overline{y} - \widetilde{y_u})\right] \equiv \lambda_u^n(1), \tag{3.48}$$

where $\overline{y} \equiv \left[(\lambda_s^n + \lambda_s^m)y_s + (\lambda_u^n + \lambda_u^m)y_u\right]/(1 + \lambda_s^m + \lambda_u^m)$.
Again, it is true that $\lambda_u^n(1) < \lambda_u^n(0)$, and we get the result of multiple political equilibria in an open economy where migrants are allowed to vote when $\lambda_u^n(1) < \lambda_u^n < \lambda_u^n(0)$.

3.A.2 One-period open economy: endogenous labour supply.

Again, the equilibrium tax rate will be zero, if

$$\lambda_u^n \leq 0.5(1 + \lambda_s^m - \lambda_u^m),$$

or, substituting for λ_s^m and λ_u^m,

$$\lambda_u^n \leq 0.5\left[1 + (\theta y_s - \varphi y_u) - (\theta\widetilde{y_s} - \varphi\widetilde{y_u})\right] \equiv \lambda_u^n(0). \tag{3.49}$$

For the equilibrium tax rate to be positive, it must be true that

$$\lambda_u^n > 0.5(1 + \lambda_s^m - \lambda_u^m),$$

and that therefore

$$\lambda_u^n > 0.5\left[1 + (1 - t^*)(\theta y_s - \varphi y_u) - (\theta\widetilde{y_s} - \varphi\widetilde{y_u}) + b^*(\theta - \varphi)\right] \equiv \tag{3.50}$$

$$\equiv \lambda_u^n(+).$$

Assuming $\theta w_s^2 - \varphi w_u^2 > 0$, it is true that $\lambda_u^n(+) < \lambda_u^n(0)$, and we get the result of multiple political equilibria in an open economy where migrants are allowed to vote when $\lambda_u^n(+) < \lambda_u^n < \lambda_u^n(0)$.

Proof.

For $\lambda_u^n(+) < \lambda_u^n(0)$, it needs to be true that

$$b^*(\theta - \varphi) - t^*(\theta y_s - \varphi y_u) < 0.$$

Using (3.12) to substitute for b^* and rearranging, we get:

$$(\theta - \varphi)t^* \left[(\lambda_s^n + \lambda_s^m)y_s + (\lambda_u^n + \lambda_u^m)y_u\right]/(1 + \lambda_s^m + \lambda_u^m) <$$

$$< t^*(\theta y_s - \varphi y_u),$$

or

$$\theta(y_s - \overline{y}) > \varphi(y_u - \overline{y}),$$

where $\overline{y} \equiv \left[(\lambda_s^n + \lambda_s^m)y_s + (\lambda_u^n + \lambda_u^m)y_u\right]/(1 + \lambda_s^m + \lambda_u^m)$. This is true since $\overline{y} < y_s$ and $\overline{y} > y_u$ and, according to our assumption, $\theta w_s^2 - \varphi w_u^2 > 0$.

Q.E.D.

3.A.3 Two-period open economy.

For a two-period open economy, we derive the same results as above, analogously.

3.B Optimal income taxation with endogenous labour supply.

In the following, optimal income taxation is derived for the case of endogenous labour supply in an open economy.

Let individual preferences be described by the following (direct) utility function

$$u(c,l) = c + l - l^2/2, \tag{3.51}$$

with consumption c and leisure l. The individual time constraint is

$$l + L = 1, \tag{3.52}$$

with work L, and the individual budget constraint is

$$c = (1-t)w_i L + b, \tag{3.53}$$

with individual pre-tax hourly wage w_i, a lump sum benefit or grant b or, using (3.52):

$$c = (1-t)w_i - (1-t)w_i l + b. \tag{3.54}$$

Substitute c in the utility function to get utility as a function of leisure:

$$u_i(l) = (1-t)w_i - (1-t)w_i l + b + l - l^2/2. \tag{3.55}$$

Solving the foc, which is

$$u_i'(l) = 1 - (1-t)w_i - l = 0, \tag{3.56}$$

for l to derive leisure demand,

$$l_i = 1 - (1-t)w_i, \tag{3.57}$$

labour supply

$$L_i = 1 - l_i = (1-t)w_i, \tag{3.58}$$

and pre-tax income:

$$y_i = (1-t)w_i^2. \tag{3.59}$$

Insert (3.57) in (3.55) to get indirect utility as a function of the tax rate and the lump sum grant $v_i(t, b)$:

$$v_i(t, b) = 0.5 + b + 0.5(1-t)^2 w_i^2. \quad (3.60)$$

Again, feasible redistribution policy must satisfy the government budget constraint (see3.12):

$$b = t[(\lambda_s^n + \lambda_s^m)y_s + (\lambda_u^n + \lambda_u^m)y_u]/(1 + \lambda_s^m + \lambda_u^m).$$

Inserting (3.59) in (3.12) yields:

$$b = t(1-t)[(\lambda_s^n + \lambda_s^m)w_s^2 + (\lambda_u^n + \lambda_u^m)w_u^2]/(1 + \lambda_s^m + \lambda_u^m). \quad (3.61)$$

Insert (3.61) in (3.60) to get indirect utility as a function of the tax rate $v_i(t)$:

$$v_i(t) = 0.5 + t(1-t)[(\lambda_s^n + \lambda_s^m)w_s^2 + (\lambda_u^n + \lambda_u^m)w_u^2]/(1 + \lambda_s^m + \lambda_u^m) + \quad (3.62)$$
$$+0.5(1-t)^2 w_i^2,$$

with the first order condition:

$$v_i'(t) = (1-2t)[(\lambda_s^n + \lambda_s^m)w_s^2 + (\lambda_u^n + \lambda_u^m)w_u^2]/(1 + \lambda_s^m + \lambda_u^m) - \quad (3.63)$$
$$-(1-t)w_i^2 = 0, \quad i = s, u.$$

Solving for t yields the optimal tax rate, that is the one which maximises indirect utility $v_i(t)$:

$$t_i^* = \frac{[(\lambda_s^n + \lambda_s^m)w_s^2 + (\lambda_u^n + \lambda_u^m)w_u^2]/(1 + \lambda_s^m + \lambda_u^m) - w_i^2}{2[(\lambda_s^n + \lambda_s^m)w_s^2 + (\lambda_u^n + \lambda_u^m)w_u^2](1 + \lambda_s^m + \lambda_u^m) + w_i^2}, \quad (3.64)$$
$$i = s, u.$$

or, using (3.59),

$$t_i^* = \frac{[(\lambda_s^n + \lambda_s^m)y_s + (\lambda_u^n + \lambda_u^m)y_u]/(1 + \lambda_s^m + \lambda_u^m) - y_i}{2[(\lambda_s^n + \lambda_s^m)y_s + (\lambda_u^n + \lambda_u^m)y_u]/(1 + \lambda_s^m + \lambda_u^m) + y_i}, \tag{3.65}$$

$$i = s, u.$$

Note that for a closed economy, where $\lambda_s^m, \lambda_u^m = 0$, we would derive analogously:

$$t_i^* = \frac{\lambda_s^n y_s + \lambda_u^n y_u - y_i}{2(\lambda_s^n y_s + \lambda_u^n y_u) + y_i}, \quad i = s, u. \tag{3.66}$$

Bibliography

Abio, G. (2003), *Is the deficit under control? A generational accounting perspective on fiscal policy and labour market trends in Spain.* Investigaciones Economicas 27/2, pp. 309-341.

Ablett, J. (1996a), *Generational accounting - an Australian perspective.* Review of Income and Wealth 42/1, pp. 91-105.

Ablett, J. (1996b), *Generational accounting and intergenerational balance.* Agenda 3/4, pp. 407-418.

Ablett, J. (1997), *A set of generational accounts for Australia: base year 1994/95.* Economic and Labour Relations Review 8/1, pp. 90-109.

Ablett, J. and Z. Tseggai-Bocurezion (2000), *Lifetime net average tax rates in Australia since federation - a generational accounting study.* Economic Record 76/233, pp. 139-151.

Accardo, J. (2002), *Une etude de comptabilite generationnelle pour la France en 1996.* (A generational accounting study for France in 1996. With English summary.). Economie et Prevision 0/154, pp. 43-57.

Akbari, A. (1989), *Benefits of immigrants to Canada: evidence on tax and public services.* Canadian Public Policy 15, pp. 424-435.

Altonji, J.G. and D. Card (1991), *The effects of immigration on the labor market outcomes of less-skilled natives.* In: J.M. Abowd and R.B. Freeman (eds.), Immigration, Trade and Labor, University of Chicago Press.

Amegashie, J.A. (2002), *A political economy model of immigration quotas.* Unpublished manuscript.

Angrist, J.D. and A.D. Kugler (2001), *Labor market institutions and the impact of immigrants on natives: evidence from Western Europe.* Unpublished manuscript.

Auerbach, A.J. (1997), *Generational accounting in New Zealand: Is there generational balance?* International Tax and Public Finance 4/2, pp. 201-28.

Auerbach, A.J. and P. Oreopoulos (1999), *Generational accounting and immigration in the United States.* NBER Working Paper 7041.

Auerbach, A.J., J. Gokhale and L. Kotlikoff (1991), *Generational accounts: a meaningful alternative to deficit accounting.* In: D. Bradford (ed.), Tax Policy and the Economy 5, Cambridge, MA.

Auerbach, A.J., J. Gokhale and L. Kotlikoff (1992), *Social security and Medicare policy from the perspective of generational accounting.* Federal Reserve Bank of Cleveland Working Paper 9206.

Auerbach, A.J., J. Gokhale and L. Kotlikoff (1994), *Generational accounts: a meaningful way to evaluate fiscal policy.* Journal of Economic Perspectives 8, pp. 73-94.

Baldwin-Edwards, M. (1991), *The socio-political rights of migrants in the EC.* In: G. Room (ed.), Towards a European Welfare State, pp. 189-234.

Baldwin-Edwards, M. (1997), *Third country nationals and welfare systems in the European Union.* Jean Monnet Working Paper in Comparative and International Politics 12.97.

Bateman, H. and J. Ablett (2000), *Compulsory superannuation and Australian generational accounts.* Economic Analysis and Policy 30/1, pp. 33-48.

Benhabib, J. (1996), *A note on the political economy of immigration.* European Economic Review 40, pp. 1737-1743.

Besendorfer, D., C. Borgmann and B. Raffelhüschen (1998), *Ein Plädoyer für intergenerative Ausgewogenheit: Rentenreformvorschläge auf dem Prüfstand.* (Addressing Intergenerational Balance: Social Security Reforms on a Yardstick. With English summary.). Ifo Studien 44/3, pp. 209-31.

Besley, T. and S. Coate (1998), *Sources of inefficiency in a representative democracy: a dynamic analysis.* The American Economic Review 88/1, pp. 139-156.

Boll, S., B. Raffelhüschen and J. Walliser (1994), *Social security and intergenerational redistribution: A Generational Accounting Perspective.* Public Choice.

Bonin, H., B. Raffelhüschen and J. Walliser (2000), *Can immigration alleviate the demographic burden?* Finanzarchiv 57.

Bonin, H. (2001), *Generational accounting - theory and application.* Springer Verlag Berlin, Heidelberg, New York.

Bonin, H., J. Gil and C. Patxot (2001), *Beyond the Toledo agreement: the intergenerational impact of the Spanish pension reform.* Spanish Economic Review 3/2, pp. 111-30.

Bonnet, C. (2002), *Comptabilite generationnelle appliquee a la France: Quelques facteurs d'instabilite des resultats.* (Using Generational Accounting for France: Some Factors of Result Instability. With English summary.). Economie et Prevision 0/154, pp. 59-78.

Borjas, G.J. (1990), *Friends or strangers: the impact of immigrants on the U.S. economy.* Basic Books, New York.

Borjas, G.J. (1993), *The impact of immigrants on employment opportunities of natives.* In: OECD, The Changing Course of International Migration, Paris.

Borjas, G.J. (1994), *The economics of immigration.* Journal of Economic Literature 32, pp. 1667-1717.

Borjas, G.J. (1995), *The economic benefits from immigration.* Journal of Economic Perspectives 9.

Borjas, G.J. (1999), *The economic analysis of immigration - immigration and the wage structure.* Handbook of Labor Economics.

Borjas, G.J. and S.J. Trejo (1991), *Immigrant participation in the welfare system.* NBER Working Paper 3423.

Borjas, G.J., R.B. Freeman and L.F. Katz (1996), *Searching for the effect of immigration on the labor market.* NBER Working Paper 5454.

Borstinghaus, V. and G. Hirte (2001), *Generational accounting versus computable general equilibrium.* FinanzArchiv 58/3, pp. 227-243.

Buiter, W.H. (1995), *Generational accounts, aggregate saving and intergenerational distribution.* CEPR Discussion Paper 237.

Bundesministerium für soziale Sicherheit und Generationen (BMSG) (1999), *Bericht über die soziale Lage.*

Burda, M. (1995), *Migration and the option value of waiting.* CEPR Discussion Paper 1229.

Card, D. (1990), *The impact of the Mariel boatlift on the Miami labor market.* Industrial and Labor Relations Review 43, pp. 245-257.

Card, D. (2001), *Immigrant inflows, native outflows and the local labor market impacts of higher immigration.* Journal of Labor Economics 19/1, pp. 22-63.

Cardarelli, R., J. Sefton and L. Kotlikoff (2000), *Generational accounting in the UK.* Economic Journal 110/467, pp. 547-574.

Casarico, A. and C. Devillanova (2003), *Social security and migration with endogenous skill upgrading.* Journal of Public Economics 87, pp. 773-797.

Cattoir, P. and F. Docquier (2000), *Debt-sharing and secession: a generational accounting approach.* CORE Discussion Paper 03.

Cesarani, D. and M. Fulbrook, eds. (1996), *Citizenship, nationality and migration in Europe.* Routledge, London and New York.

Clune, M. (1997), *The fiscal impacts of immigrants: a California case study.* Department of Demography, University of California, Berkeley.

Coppel, J., J.C. Dumont and I. Visco (2001), *Trends in immigration and economic consequences.* OECD Economic Department Working Paper 284.

Cremer, H. and P. Pestieau (1998), *Social insurance, majority voting and labor mobility.* Journal of Public Economics 68, pp. 397-420.

Cremer, H. and P. Pestieau (2002), *Factor mobility and redistribution.* Unpublished manuscript.

Cukierman, A., Z. Hercowitz and D. Pines (1993), *The political economy of immigration.* Tel Aviv Foerder Institute for Economic Research Working Paper 17/93.

DeNew, J.P. and K.F. Zimmermann (1994), *Native wage impacts of foreign labour: a random effects panel analysis.* Journal of Population Economics 7/2.

Diamond, P. (1996), *Generational accounts and generational balance: an assessment.* National Tax Journal 49/4, pp. 597-607.

Docquier, F., P. Liegeois and J.P. Stijns (1999), *Comptabilite generationnelle et vieillissement demographique: Les enseignements d'un modele dequilibre general calculable calibre pour la Belgique.* (Generational Accounting and the Aging of the Population: A Computable General Equilibrium Approach for Belgium. With English summary.). L'Actualite Economique/ Revue D'Analyse Economique 75/1-3, pp. 333-356.

Dolmas, J. and G.W. Huffman (2003), *On the political economy of immigration and income redistribution.* Working Paper 03/12, Department of Economics, Vanderbilt University.

Dustmann, C. and I. Preston (2000), *Racial and economic factors in attitudes to immigration.* CEPR Discussion Paper 2542.

Dustmann, C., F. Fabbri, I. Preston and J. Wadsworth (2003), *The local labour market effects of immigration in the UK.* Home Office Online Report 06.

Epstein, G. and S. Nitzan (2002), *The struggle over migration policy.* CEPR Discussion Paper 3466.

EUROPA, Justice and Home Affairs, *European Union citizenship, European Union rights.* http://europa.eu.int/comm/justice home/fsj/citizenship/fsj citizenship intro en.htm as of Jan 31, 2003.

European Commission (1999), *Generational accounting in Europe.* European Economy 6.

Eurostat (1999), *European Community Household Panel (ECHP) Wave 5, 6 (Austrian Wave 4, 5).*

Fehr, H. and L. Kotlikoff (1995), *Generational accounting in general equilibrium.* NBER Working Paper 5090.

Felder, S. (1997), *Vom "Deficit Accounting" zum "Generational Accounting": Eine Anwendung für die Schweiz.* (With English summary.). Schweizerische Zeitschrift für Volkswirtschaft und Statistik/Swiss Journal of Economics and Statistics 133/3, pp. 497-511.

Fisher, E. and K. Kasa (1997), *Generational accounting in open economies.* Federal Reserve Bank of San Francisco Economic Review 0/3, pp. 34-46.

Flores, O. (1997), *The political economy of immigration quotas.* Atlantic Economic Journal 25/1.

Friedberg, R.M. and J. Hunt (1995), *The impact of immigrants on host country wages, employment and growth.* Journal of Economic Perspectives 9/2, pp. 23-44.

Gal, R.I. and G. Tarcali (2003), *Pension reform and intergenerational redistribution in Hungary.* Unpublished manuscript.

Garvey, D. and T. Espenshade (1996), *Fiscal impacts of New Jersey's immigrant and native households on state and local governments: a new approach and new estimates.* Office of Population Research, Princeton University.

Gjersem, C.E. (2002), *A presentation of generational accounting in Norway.* Nordic Journal of Political Economy 28/1, pp. 61-73.

Gokhale, J., B. Raffelhüschen and J. Walliser (1995), *The burden of German unification: a generational accounting approach.* In: FinanzArchiv 52/2, pp. 141-165.

Greenwood, M.J. and J.M. McDowell (1986), *The factor market consequences of U.S. immigration.* Journal of Economic Literature 24/4, pp. 1738-1772.

Grether, J., J. deMelo and T. Müller (2000), *The political economy of international migration in a Ricardo-Viner model.* Cahier de recherche en conomie politique CR-E-00-03.

Gross, D.M. (1999), *Three million foreigners, three million unemployed? Immigration and the French labour market.* IMF Working Paper 99/124.

Gustaffson, B. and T. Osterberg (2001), *Immigrants and the public sector budget: accounting exercises for Sweden.* Journal of Population Economics 14, pp. 689-708.

Hagemann, R.P. and C. John (1997), *Fiscal reform in Sweden: what generational accounting tells us.* Contemporary Economic Policy 15/3, pp. 1-12.

Haupt, A. and W. Peters (1998), *Public pensions and voting on immigration.* Public Choice 95, pp. 403-413.

Hauptverband der österreichischen Sozialversicherungsträger (1999), *Statistisches Handbuch der österreichischen Sozialversicherung.*

Hougaard, J. and B. Raffelhüschen (1997), *Generational and gender-specific aspects of the tax and transfer system in Denmark.* Empirical Economics 22/4, pp. 615-35.

Hunt, J. (1992), *The impact of the 1962 repatriates from Algeria on the French labor market.* Industrial and Labor Relations Review 45/3, pp. 556-572.

Issac, J. (1947), *Economics of migration.* Routledge, London.

Jaeger, D.A. (1996), *Skill differences and the effect of immigrants on the wages of natives.* Working Paper 273, Bureau of Labor Statistics, U.S. Department of Labor.

Joppke, C., ed. (1998), *Challenge to the nation-state - immigration in Western Europe and the United States.* Oxford University Press.

Kemnitz, A. (2002), *On the political economy of low skilled immigration and the welfare state.* International Tax and Public Finance 9, pp. 423-434.

Keuschnigg, C., M. Keuschnigg, R. Koman, E. Lüth and B. Raffelhüschen (1999), *Austria: restoring generational balance.* In: European Commission (1999), Generational accounting in Europe. European Economy Number 6.

Keuschnigg, C., M. Keuschnigg, R. Koman, E. Lüth, and B. Raffelhüschen (2000) Public debt and generational balance in Austria. Empirica 27, pp. 225-252.

Kotlikoff, L.J. (1992), *Generational Accounting.* Macmillan, USA.

Kotlikoff, L. (1993), *From deficit delusion to the fiscal balance rule - looking for a sensible way to measure fiscal policy.* Journal of Economics 7 (suppl.), pp. 17-41.

Kotlikoff, L. and B. Raffelhüschen (1999), *Generational accounting around the globe.* American Economic Review 89/2, pp. 161-66.

Kotlikoff, L. and W. Leibfritz (1998), *An international comparison of generational accounts.* NBER Working Paper 6447.

Kotlikoff, L.J. (2001), *Generational policy.* NBER Working Paper 8163.

Krieger, T. (2003), *Voting on low-skill immigration under different pension regimes.* Public Choice 117, pp. 51-78.

Kuhn, P. and I. Wooton (1991), *Immigration, international trade and the wages of native workers.* In: J.M. Abowd and R.B. Freeman (eds.), Immigration, Trade and Labor. University of Chicago Press.

Lalonde, R.J. and R.H. Topel (1991), *Labor market adjustment to increased immigration.* In: J.M. Abowd and R.B. Freeman (eds.), Immigration, Trade and Labor. University of Chicago Press.

Layton-Henry, Z., ed. (1990), *The political rights of migrant workers in Western Europe.* SAGE Modern Politics Series 25, London, Newbury Park, New Delhi.

Lehner, G. (1999), *Bund schöpft 1998 Defizitquote nicht aus.* Wifo Monatsberichte 5.

Lejour, A.M. and H.A. Verbon (1994), *Labour mobility and decision making on social insurance in an integrated market.* Public Choice 79, pp. 161-185.

Levy, J. and O. Dore (1998), *Generational accounting for France.* International Monetary Fund Working Paper 98/14.

MaCurdy, T., T. Nechyba and J. Bhattacharya (1996), *An economic framework for assessing the fiscal impacts of immigration.* Department of Economics, Stanford University.

Malvar, R.V. and L. Kotlikoff (1997), *Balanco intergeracional: O caso brasileiro.* (With English summary.). Pesquisa e Planejamento Economico 27/3, pp. 493-518.

Mazza, I. and F. van Winden (1996), *A political economic analysis of labor migration and income redistribution.* Public Choice 88, pp. 333-363.

Mazzaferro, C. (2000), *I conti generazionali e la sostenibilita della politica fiscale.* (Generational Accounting and Fiscal Policy Sustainability. With English summary.). Economia Politica 17/3, pp. 469-508.

Murphy, M.C. and J.L. Beard (1996), *Assessing fiscal policies via generational accounting and opportunity costs.* Journal of Private Enterprise 12/1, pp. 89-107.

Oates, W. (1972), *Fiscal federalism.* Gregg Revivals, Aldershot, England.

OECD (1994), *Trends in international migration.* Sopemi Annual Report 1994.

OECD (1997), *Trends in international migration.* Sopemi Annual Report 1996.

Oreopoulos, P. (1996), *A generational accounting perspective on Canadian public policy.* University of British Columbia Department of Economics Discussion Paper 96/12.

Österreichische Nationalbank (2003), Statistisches Monatsheft, *Staatsquoten - Struktur der Einnahmen.* Tabelle 5.4.0, http://www2.oenb.at/stat-monatsheft/tabellen/540p.htm 2003.

Österreichische Nationalbank, Staatsschuldenausschuss (2000), *Bericht über die Finanzschuld des Bundes 1999.* Wien.

Pischke, J. and J. Velling (1997), *Employment effects of immigration to Germany: an analysis based on local labor markets.* The Review of Economics and Statistics.

Poschner, Hans (1996), *Die Effekte der Migration auf die soziale Sicherung.* Universität Regensburg (Dissertation), Weiden.

Raffelhüschen, B. (1999a), *Generational accounting in Europe.* American Economic Review 89/2, pp. 167-70.

Raffelhüschen, B. (1999b), *Generational accounting: method, data and limitations.* In: European Commission (1999), Generational accounting in Europe. European Economy 6.

Raffelhüschen, B. and A.E. Risa (1997), *Generational accounting and intergenerational welfare.* Public Choice 93/1-2, pp. 149-63.

Razin, A. and E. Sadka (1995), *Resisting migration: wage rigidity and income redistribution.* American Economic Review, Papers and Proceedings 85, pp. 312-316.

Razin, A. and E. Sadka (1997), *Tax burden and migration: a political economy perspective.* IMF Working Paper 97/78.

Razin, A. and E. Sadka (1999a), *Unskilled migration: a burden or a boon for the welfare state.* NBER Working Paper 7013.

Razin, A. and E. Sadka (1999b), *Migration and pension with international capital mobility.* Journal of Public Economics 74, pp. 141-150.

Razin, A., E. Sadka and P. Swagel (2002), *Tax burden and migration: a political economy theory and evidence.* Journal of Public Economics 85, pp. 167-190.

Riedel, M. and M.M. Hofmarcher (2001), *Effects of ageing on health expenditure.* Institute for Advanced Studies, Vienna.

Rothman, E.S. and T.J. Espenshade (1992), *Fiscal impacts of immigration to the United States.* Population Index 58/3, pp. 381-415.

Sarrapy, C.S. and L.V. Caso (1999), *The long-run sustainability of fiscal policy in Mexico: a generational accounting approach.* Economia Mexicana, Nueva Epoca 8/2, pp. 367-403.

Scholten, U. and M. Thum (1996), *Public pension and immigration policy in a democracy.* Public Choice 66, pp. 347-361.

Shugart, W.F., R.D. Tollison and M. Kimenyi (1986), *The political economy of immigration restrictions.* Yale Journal of Regulation 4, pp. 79-97.

Simon, J. (1984), *Immigrants, taxes and welfare in the United States.* Population and Development Review 10, pp. 55-69.

Simon, J. (1989), *The economic consequences of immigration.* Basil Blackwell, Oxford.

Sinn, H.W. (2002), *EU enlargement and the future of the welfare state.* Scottish Journal of Political Economy 49, pp. 104-115.

Smith, J.P. and B. Edmonston, eds., (1997), *The new Americans - economic, demographic and fiscal effects of immigration.* National Academy Press, Washington, D.C.

Söllner, F. (1999), *A note on the political economy of immigration.* Public Choice 100, pp. 245-251.

Soysal, Y. (1994), *Limits of citizenship: migrants and postnational membership in Europe.* University of Chicago Press, Chicago.

Statistik Austria (1999), *Krippen, Kindergärten und Horte (Kindertagesheime) - Berichtsjahr 1998/99.* Heft 1308.

Statistik Austria (2000), *Mikrozensus Jahresergebnisse 1998.* Heft 1328 (Tabelle 106).

Statistik Austria (2000), *Österreichische Hochschulstatistik - Studienjahr 1998/99.* Heft 1355.

Statistik Austria (2001a), *Statistische Nachrichten 11/2001.*

Statistik Austria (2001b), *Statistische Nachrichten 12/2001.*

Statistik Austria (2002), *MWST-Vorgaben 2000 für die VGR Jahresrechnung Privater Konsum.* Provided by Mr Bernhard Mazegger on request.

Statistik Austria (2002), *Bildungsausgaben des Staates 1995 bis 1999.* http://www.statistik.at, as of August 16, 2002.

Statistik Austria (2003a), *Bevölkerung Österreichs im 21. Jahrhundert.* ftp://www.statistik.at/pub/neuerscheinungen/ bev21jhdt web.pdf as of 17 October, 2003.

Statistik Austria (2003b), *Demographisches Jahrbuch 2001/2002.*

Statistik Austria (2003c), *Statistische Übersichten.* http://www.statistik.at/statistische uebersichten/deutsch/pdf/ indikato.pdf, as of January 5, 2004.

Stijns, J.P. (2002), *Comptabilite generationnelle belge. (Generational Accounting in Belgium. With English summary.)* Economie et Prevision 0/154, pp. 31-41.

Storesletten, K. (2000), *Sustaining fiscal policy through immigration.* Journal of Political Economy, 108/2.

Takayama, N. and F. Arita (1995), *How is per-capita disposable income divided between generations in Japan?* (In Japanese. With English summary.). Economic Review (Keizai Kenkyu) 46/1, pp. 43-58.

Takayama, N. and Y. Kitamura (1999), *Lessons from generational accounting in Japan.* American Economic Review 89/2, pp. 171-175.

Tamura, Y. (2003), *Referendum-led immigration policy in the welfare state.* Unpublished manuscript.

Ter Rele, H. (1998), *Generational accounts for the Dutch public sector.* De Economist 146/4, pp. 555-584.

Ulrich, R. (1992), *Der Einfluss der Zuwanderung auf die staatlichen Einnahmen und Ausgaben in Deutschland.* In: Buttler, G., H.J. Hoffmann-Nowotny, G. Schmitt-Rink (eds.), Acta Demographica. Heidelberg, pp. 189-208.

Van Heerden, J.H. and N.J. Schoeman (2000), *Generational accounting: a comparison between various taxes' incidence on the young and old in South Africa.* Journal for Studies in Economics and Econometrics 24/2, pp. 35-51.

Vanne, R. (2002), *The Finnish generational accounting revisited.* Nordic Journal of Political Economy 28/1, pp. 13-25.

Vernez, G. and K. McCarthy (1995), *The fiscal costs of immigration: analytical and policy issues.* The Rand Center.

Vernez, G. and K. McCarthy (1996), *The mixed economic progress of immigrants.* RAND/MR-763.

Vishwanath, T. (1991), *Information flow, job search and migration.* Journal of Development Economics 36/2.

Wellisch, D. and D.E. Wildasin (1996), *Decentralized income redistribution and immigration.* European Economic Review 40, pp. 187-217.

Wellisch, D. and U. Walz (1998), *Why do rich countries prefer free trade over free migration? The role of the modern welfare state.* European Economic Review 42, pp. 1595-1612.

WIFO, *Wirtschaftsdaten.* http://www.wifo.ac.at/cgi-bin/tabellen/transtb2.cgi?3++staat.d+++++0+4000, as of September 2003.

Wildasin, D.E. (1994), *Income redistribution and migration.* Canadian Journal of Economics 27, pp. 637-656.

Winkelmann, R. and K.F. Zimmermann (1993), *Ageing, migration and labour mobility.* In: Johnson, P. and KF. Zimmermann (eds.), Labour Markets in an Ageing Europe. Cambridge University Press, pp. 255-283.

Winter-Ebmer, R. and J. Zweimüller (1996), *Immigration and the earnings of young native workers.* Oxford Economics Papers 48, pp. 473-491.

Winter-Ebmer, R. and J. Zweimüller (1999), *Do immigrants displace young native workers: the Austrian experience.* Journal of Population Economics 12/2, pp. 327-340.

Wodak, R. (2000), *Discourses of exclusion: a European comparative study.* Speech at the Opening of the EU Observatorium, Hofburg Vienna. http://www.oeaw.ac.at/wittgenstein/racism/EuObservatoriumkurz.htm as of Jan 31, 2003.

Peter Lang · Europäischer Verlag der Wissenschaften

Ingo Tschach

The Theory of Development Finance

How Microcredit Programmes Alleviate Credit and Labour Market Segmentation

Frankfurt am Main, Berlin, Bern, Bruxelles, New York, Oxford, Wien, 2002.
XIII, 160 pp., 64 fig., 3 tab.
Development and Finance.
Edited by Manfred Nitsch, Reinhard H. Schmidt and Claus Peter Zeitinger. Vol. 11
ISBN 3-631-39203-6 / US-ISBN 0-8204-5493-1 · pb. € 39.–*

The book explores the problem of credit market segmentation, a widespread phenomenon in developing countries, within a theoretical framework based on graphical analysis. It investigates the causes and effects of this problem, and the impact of possible solutions. Credit market segmentation is an outgrowth of information-related problems and high transaction costs in lending. It leads to segmentation in labour markets and also results in inefficient factor allocation and highly skewed income distribution patterns. A theoretical impact analysis shows that microcredit programmes can eliminate the causes and effects of credit market segmentation and that their impact is much broader than is usually assumed. This book should be required reading for everyone who is interested in microcredit.

Contents: The Theoretical Derivation of Credit Market Segmentation · The Impacts of Credit Market Segmentation · Approaches Taken by Successful Small Loan Programmes · Impact Analysis of Small Loan Programmes: How They Affect Financial Markets, Labour Markets, Factor Allocation, Income Distribution and Growth

Kolibri 360 GmbH
Ferdinand-Jühlke-Straße 7
99095 Erfurt, Deutschland
produktsicherheit@kolibri360.de

Druck:
CPI Druckdienstleistungen GmbH
im Auftrag der
Kolibri 360 GmbH
Ferdinand-Jühlke-Str. 7
99095 Erfurt